NATURE GUIDE TO THE CAROLINA COAST

COMMON BIRDS, CRABS, SHELLS, FISH, AND OTHER ENTITIES OF THE COASTAL ENVIRONMENT

Revere the Earth!

by
Peter Meyer

AVIAN-CETACEAN
PRESS

Printed and bound in the United States of America. Published by Avian-Cetacean Press in Wilmington, NC.

Cover Photos: Ghost Crab, Brown Pelican, Coquina Clams around a shark's tooth, Sheepshead.

All diagrams and photographs, unless otherwise credited, are by the author.

Seventh Printing, 2001; text revised: 1994, 1998, 2000

Comments and suggestions are welcome; send communications to the author, c/o Avian-Cetacean Press, PO Box 15643, Wilmington, NC 28408.

ISBN 0-9628186-0-7

Library of Congress Catalog Card Number 90-85396

Dedication

Nature Guide is dedicated to my family. Cathy, Ben (4), and Jason (2) have accompanied me on countless "messing about" expeditions in our boat, the **Tern.** Fortunately, they enjoy exploring the waterways and backwater areas as much as I. My appreciation and love to you, my fellow Sound Rats.

Disclaimer

The author presents opinions on the edibility of marine fauna and flora in *Nature Guide*. Readers should form independent opinions about the safety of eating the species discussed; extreme caution should be taken in consuming species which are potentially toxic.

Acknowledgments

Special thanks to manuscript reviewers: Dr. Anne McCrary (UNCW Professor), Mrs. Alta VanLandingham (NC Shell Club), Mr. Fritz Rohde (NC Marine Fisheries), Mr. Walker Golder (manager of Audubon Society's NC coastal island sanctuary system), Mr. Andy Wood (NC Aquarium).

*Mr. Paul Barrington (NC Aquarium) kindly provided specimens to photograph. Dr. Richard Bird, Mr. Bob Slaughter, and Dr. James Parnell provided the superb bird photographs in **Nature Guide**.*

Wordwright Publishing of Wilmington, NC, provided essential assistance in typesetting.

*"He was a bold man
that first eat an oyster."*
— *Jonathan Swift*

Table of Contents

FISH 67

OTHERS 89

COASTAL ENVIRONMENT 109

SEAFOOD 129

AUTHOR'S COMMENTS 133

NATURE GUIDE TO THE CAROLINA COAST

The Blue Whale is the largest animal
ever *to inhabit the earth,*
far larger than any dinosaur.

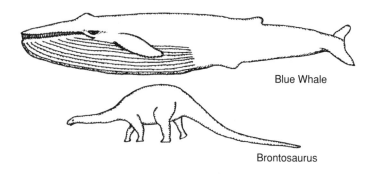

Blue Whale

Brontosaurus

INTRODUCTION

Nature Guide to the Carolina Coast is a <u>practical</u> guide to the common birds, crabs, shells, fish, other animals, and environment of the Carolina coast. The book is designed as an entertaining, informative, easy-to-read reference for coastal residents and visitors alike. Indeed, anyone who enjoys beachcombing will learn from the *Nature Guide*.

The text uses common names (instead of scientific names) to identify plants and animals; non-scientist readers can more easily assimilate common names.

Nature Guide to the Carolina Coast is not an all-encompassing, rigid scientific volume. The information presented, however, is extensive and as accurate as possible.

The *Nature Guide* will be useful to anyone interested in the coastal environment. The book can be used outdoors, during activities such as beachcombing, hiking, or fishing. There, *Nature Guide* serves as a field guide for identifying common coastal specimens. The text can also be read indoors, at the reader's leisure; specific information about common coastal entities is presented in each section of the book.

Dredge-spoil islands provide nesting habitat crucial to supporting coastal bird populations.

BIRDS

Birds — what is it about them that fascinates us so? Perhaps it is birds' similarities to humans and other mammals: Like us, birds are warm-blooded vertebrates. Or is it birds' mastery of flight that enamors us? Many among us dream of flying like a bird. Perhaps the beautiful and varied feather patterns of birds just please our eye? Or maybe humans anthropomorphize, giving birds human-like qualities: It is easy to think of birds as clean, sharp, capable, parental, etc.

While the specific attributes that attract us to birds are elusive, the characteristics that set birds apart are clear: Birds are animals with a backbone, are homeothermic (warm-blooded), and possess wings and feathers.

Feathers, more than anything else, define birds. Only birds have feathers, and it is feathers which make birds masters of the air. Just as fur is distinctive and important to mammals, so are feathers to birds.

Feathers are made of keratin, the same substance of human nails and reptiles' scales (not surprising, as birds evolved from reptile-like ancestors). On either side of the central shaft of a feather are a hundred or more filaments. Each filament is similarly composed of numerous smaller filaments or barbules. The smaller elements overlap in different ways, depending on the function of the feather.

The functions of feathers are many.

The most obvious function of feathers is flight. Other animals glide, and a few, like bats and insects, fly well — but birds are the true masters of flight.

Feathers further serve birds in the same manner as fur serves mammals — as insulation. Feathers actually provide better insulation than fur and are crucial in maintaining the temperature of warm-blooded birds.

Feathers keep birds dry; feathers, combined with bird oils, are waterproof.

And, finally, the colors and patterns of feathers serve in camouflage, territorial displays, and sexual identification and attraction.

In addition to wings and feathers, birds have adapted to flight in other ways. Avian bones are thin and hollow to minimize weight. Similarly, birds have lost the heavy jaws and teeth of their reptilian ancestors. And, all birds lay eggs; to carry developing young would hinder flight.

But, benefits are not without risks. Because they are warm-blooded, birds must incubate their eggs; they cannot bury their eggs and leave them, like reptiles. And, while sitting on the nest, birds are vulnerable to enemies.

Birds have adapted in other ways to succeed. The beaks of birds vary greatly in size and shape, depending on the diet of each species. Consider the differences in just the birds common to the Carolina coast: The thin bill of the tiny Sanderling is used to probe the sand for Mole Crabs. The huge beak of the Pelican, with its loose sac of skin underneath, sucks in small fish when the Pelican dives. The unique beak of the Skimmer, the lower half longer than the upper, skims the water and snaps up surface fish.

Similarly, the feet of birds vary in function, and thus in size and shape. Again, consider only the differences in a few coastal Carolina birds: The webbed feet of the Cormorant are used to swim on and below the water. The sharp-taloned feet of the Osprey are used to snatch live fish from the water. The Great Blue Heron, having huge feet with four long, thin toes, is stabilized on the marsh mud.

Whatever the overall appeal of birds is, the species of the Carolina coast have a large allotment of this allure. Few can deny the magic and enjoyment of watching our widely-varied species. The following sections discuss the more common birds that "make their living" on the Carolina coast.

BLACK SKIMMER

pictures 1, 2

The Black Skimmer is an elegant bird, quite striking in appearance and behavior. Its unique feeding habits are what make it most noticeable and distinctive.

The Skimmer catches its food by flying just above the water with its lower bill cutting the surface. When the bird hits an object with its beak, its upper jaw snaps down and grabs hold; if it is a fish, the bird feeds. If the object is a stick or such, the bird lets go. An upper movable jaw and a longer lower bill are adaptations enabling the bird to feed while skimming.

The Skimmer can be seen feeding in waters of both the sound and the ocean surf zone. While it feeds more often in the early evening and night, it can also be seen feeding during the day. Fish, shrimp, and other crustaceans on the water's surface are eaten.

A contrasting black topside and white underside make the Skimmer stand out. Long wings and a large red bill (black-tipped) are also distinctive. The legs of the Skimmer are red.

Skimmers are ground nesters. The birds nest on bare sand or sparsely-vegetated sandy locations. In years past, Skimmers had ample nesting sites on open beaches. With increasing oceanfront development and off-road vehicle traffic, however, the birds lost many nesting areas. Skimmers still nest on protected barrier beaches; in addition, they have adapted to nest on sandy dredge-spoil islands created by man.

A Skimmer nest consists of a simple bowl-shaped hollow in the sand. The tan eggs are typically marked by dark splotches. Adult birds will often feign injury if the nest is disturbed.

BROWN PELICAN
picture 3

How can a bird be awkward and ungainly, yet graceful and spectacular? How can a bird bring to mind ancient pterodactyls, yet easily master both sky and water? The Brown Pelican is/does all of these; Pelicans are a true delight to watch flying and feeding.

Brown Pelicans are huge birds, with wingspans of six to seven feet. The

birds are light for their size, though, reaching a maximum weight of about eight pounds (compare the size of a mature Pelican and a newborn human, both weighing near eight pounds).

A Pelican's beak is long and solid; its feet are large and webbed. The mature bird has a gray-brown body with a distinct white head; the immature bird is dull brown above, lighter below (the head is not white).

Brown Pelicans inhabit only coastal areas, feeding exclusively on live marine fish. Small fish such as Menhaden and Mullet make up a large part of Pelicans' diets, though they sometimes swallow one- to two-pound fish whole.

Feeding Pelicans are a wonder to observe. They fly above the water, at heights up to 50 feet; they may flap their wings or just glide along, looking for fish below the surface. Suddenly, tucking in their wings, they dive sharply for the water.

Diving Pelicans hit the surface bill-first, often making a splash. As they go beneath the surface, a large pouch from the bottom beak and throat area expands, sucking in as much as 2.5 gallons of water and (hopefully) small fish. The water is forced out through narrow gaps in the sides of the bill. If fish remain, the Pelican sits on the water and gulps down its catch. If

7

unsuccessful, the bird takes off and begins again.

Air sacs located under Pelicans' skin cushion the bird from the impact of hitting the water. The air sacs also bring the Pelican quickly to the surface.

Pelicans are also commonly seen standing on pilings or sandbars, or just sitting on the water. At times, they can be observed flying in small flocks; they may fly in a line, a foot or two above the water, or in a V-formation higher in the sky. Sometimes, semi-tame Pelicans can be found begging for fish on docks or fishing piers.

Interestingly, mature Brown Pelicans are largely silent; adult birds infrequently utter a sound, and then only a low grunt. Young birds still in the nest are vocal, squawking loudly for food.

The presence of Pelicans along the coast is sporadic. They are more common near their nesting sites, which are located exclusively on uninhabited coastal islands. There, they nest in large colonies. Bulky nests of sticks, grasses, and debris are located on the ground or in low shrubs. Unfortunately, due to coastal development, available nesting sites have been reduced in number.

Baby Pelicans are born featherless, blind, and helpless. Parent birds take turns shading the babies with their bodies. The young birds are initially fed regurgitated fish from their parents' pouches. By ten to twelve days, the baby birds are covered with white down feathers. By about nine weeks of age, the immature birds begin flying from the nest.

The population of Pelicans along the East Coast declined sharply in past years. At one time, their numbers dwindled to the point that they were placed on the Endangered Species List.

The Pelican population reduction was likely due to pesticide (DDT) residues in fish the Pelicans fed upon. High pesticide levels in females caused them to lay thin, fragile eggs, resulting in high mortality before hatching. Appropriately, the offending pesticides have been banned (at least in the U.S.).

The Brown Pelican population on the Carolina coast has increased steadily from 1974 to 1990. The Brown Pelican has been removed from the Federal Endangered Species List in the Carolinas (remains listed other locations). The birds are still protected by federal and state laws.

Pelicans are more abundant in the Carolinas during the warmer months of the year, with good reason. Pelicans nest here in the summertime and remain during temperate months. Most birds journey south to spend the winter in Florida, though some birds spend the entire year here.

CORMORANT
picture 4

The Double-crested Cormorant is found on estuary and sound waters. Most noticeable about the bird is its diving behavior; it is frequently seen swimming on the water, diving for fish. Cormorants are also seen perched on pilings or docks, drying their wings.

Like terns and Ospreys, the Cormorant is strictly piscivorous (fish-eating). Unlike terns and Ospreys, which dive from the air to feed, Cormorants dive from the surface of the water. After submerging, a Cormorant swims actively to catch its fish dinner.

The Cormorant is well-adapted for this feeding behavior, with webbed feet and a less-buoyant body. Most water birds have waterproof feathers: Air is trapped beneath the feathers, excluding moisture. The Cormorant's feathers are not waterproof, however, and air is not trapped under the feathers. As a result, the Cormorant is less buoyant and can dive more easily. At the same time, a Cormorant must periodically perch, spread its wings, and dry its feathers.

Both the webbed feet and the wings of a Cormorant propel the bird underwater. In tight places, among seaweed or rocks, only the feet are used. In open water, a Cormorant flaps its wings, "flying" underwater.

The entertaining feeding habits of the Cormorant more than make up for its somewhat drab appearance. The bird is uniformly dark in color, except for an orange throat pouch. The bird's long bill is hooked downward at the tip. The two crests on the head (for which it is named) are rarely visible. The immature Cormorant is light-breasted, and brownish on the rest of its body.

Unlike many other coastal Carolina birds, Cormorants do not nest on barrier beaches or estuarine islands. Cormorants typically nest farther north, though some lakeside nesting sights are present in the Carolinas.

Groups of Cormorants are commonly seen in the fall, migrating south. Thousands of birds pass into and through the Carolinas, often flying in V-shaped formations (like geese).

A single Cormorant will occasionally be seen swimming with its body submerged and only its snake-like neck sticking out of the water. Also unusual is the Cormorant's habit of perching in a standing-upright position.

EGRETS
pictures 5, 6

Egrets often supply Carolina beachgoers with their first glimpse of interesting coastal wildlife. Many highways to our beaches go through marshes. While driving on these roads, splashes of white in the marsh, contrasting sharply with the green-brown background, catch one's eye. Upon closer inspection, the white splashes prove to be egrets, stately birds wading gracefully through the marsh to feed.

Visitors and residents alike marvel at the elegant beauty of these birds. In marshy areas, there are two species: Snowy and Great Egrets (the Great Egret is sometimes called the Common Egret).

Both egret species have bright white plumage. The Great is 50 percent larger than the Snowy, but size alone may not differentiate the birds. However, the SNOWY EGRET is characterized by **yellow feet**, with black legs and black beak. The GREAT EGRET, on the other hand, has a **yellow bill**, with black legs and black feet.

One way to remember the difference in egrets is to think of the Snowy Egret as having yellow feet from standing in yellow-tinged snow. The other one, the Great, has the yellow beak. So, if one can see either a yellow beak, or yellow feet, egrets can be told apart instantly.

Egrets, like herons, have long legs, necks, and bills, adapted for wading in shallow water and feeding on aquatic animals. Typically, egrets are seen walking slowly and gracefully, stopping at times to stalk their food. Almost invisibly fast, an egret thrusts its head forward, snapping at prey with its beak. Egrets consume small fish, crabs, shrimp, and other animals.

Both species of egret were hunted to near-extinction in the late 1800's. Egret feathers were in great demand as decorations on women's hats. Fortunately, conservationists succeeded in passing laws protecting these birds, and egret populations have rebounded to decent levels.

Great and Snowy Egrets are also alike in nesting behavior. Both species nest in colonies, called heronries. Typically, heronries are mixed colonies of heron, egret, and ibis species. Heronries are now most often located on man-made, dredge-spoil islands. Only well-vegetated islands with dense growths of shrubs and trees are used. The stick-platform nests are placed anywhere from ground level to the very tops of trees.

Colonies of nesting birds can sometimes be spotted from sounds or the intracoastal waterway, standing out as distinct groups of large white birds gathered in trees. The heronries should not be disturbed: If intruded upon, young birds can become excited and fall from the nests; most often, the juvenile birds are stranded on the ground and perish.

The Cattle Egret is another species seen on the coast, especially in summer. These birds feed on insects, so they are not seen in the water but are found in fields, or beside highways or even airport runways. Cattle

Egrets also consume frogs, lizards, mice, and small snakes. In the breeding season, Cattle Egrets have yellow legs and beaks, and orange patches on their heads, breasts and backs.

GULLS

pictures 7, 8, 9

"Seagulls" are the most abundant and visible coastal birds, whatever season of the year. Gulls predominate because they are remarkably successful at adapting to different habitats. Their adaptability stems from not being highly specialized in function or diet. Gulls are excellent fliers, adequate walkers, and capable swimmers. Their diet is widely varied; gulls can survive on whatever food nature offers.

The general makeup of a gull consists of a heavy body, webbed feet, long pointed wings, a short square tail, and a stout bill with a slight hook at the end. Adult gulls are marked with distinct patterns of black, white, and gray; male and female gulls differ little in appearance. Immature birds are generally brownish in color; they take two to four years to attain adult plumage. Immature gulls of different species are often difficult to tell apart.

The behavior of gulls follows certain patterns as well. Groups of gulls gather quickly at feeding sites, called there by the first gulls on the scene. Gulls are primarily scavengers, but they also prey on small fish, crabs, and insects. The scavenging habit of gulls not only provides food for gulls, it also helps clean our beaches.

Unlike terns, gulls rarely dive from the air into water to feed on fish; gulls will, however, land on the surface to seize a scrap of food. In flight, gulls can soar effortlessly or flap their wings and fly strongly.

Generally, gulls nest in large colonies of their own species. Adults feed young birds by regurgitating food onto the ground.

Up to fifteen gull species have been identified in the Carolinas; all but five of these species can be classified as rarely sighted. Three species are especially common and can be characterized by their appearance and behavior.

The LAUGHING GULL is distinguished by its **black head**; it is the only common black-headed gull in the Carolinas. In the wintertime, its head molts to mostly white; as the Laughing Gull is not frequently seen here in winter, this change is not so important in identification. The bill of this species is dark red.

The Laughing Gull is talkative and noisy, calling loudly while flying or perched. The call of the Laughing Gull can be described as a series of loud, high-pitched laughs (thus its name).

Laughing Gull

The Laughing Gull seldom ventures far from salt water; it is rarely seen inland. The Laughing Gull has a habit of following ferry boats, begging for food. A less charming habit of this species is its propensity to steal eggs and young from nests of Common Terns and other birds. Laughing Gull nests are, in turn, robbed by Herring Gulls.

The HERRING GULL is a **large**, heavy bird, **pink-legged**, with a **red spot on its lower beak**; these traits distinguish it from the Ring-billed Gull.

The Herring Gull is so abundant and far-ranging that it is often referred to as the typical "seagull." The immature bird is brownish; its feather pattern, large size, and soaring flight give the young bird an almost hawk-like appearance at times. The adult Herring Gull red spot has a white head and chest, black wing tips, and gray mantle (back and upper wing surfaces). Herring Gulls eat practically anything, including fish, crabs, clams, bugs, berries, and food scraps. They range inland, often gathering to feed at trash dumps.

Herring Gull

An interesting behavior of the Herring Gull is the method it uses to open clams and other mollusks. Snatching up a clam, a Herring Gull flies off with it, then drops the clam over a hard surface, such as a highway or rocks. The bird must drop the clam from high enough to break it, but not so high that another gull can sneak in and steal the opened clam before it gets there.

The Herring Gull, like the Laughing Gull, is loud and talkative. Unlike the Laughing Gull, the Herring Gull is common in the Carolinas during the winter, less common in the summer.

The Herring Gull is an excellent flier; its aerial acrobatics provide entertainment for coastal visitors and residents alike.

The RING-BILLED GULL is the third common gull of the Carolinas. The characteristic feature of this medium-sized gull is a **black band encircling its beak** near the tip. Like the Herring Gull, it is white, with a gray mantle and black wing tips; however, the Ring-billed Gull is smaller than the Herring Gull. Its bill is yellow, and its legs are greenish-yellow.

Ring-billed Gull

The range of the Ring-billed Gull is enormous; it is common on the coast but appears throughout most of the North American Continent.

Ring-billed Gulls do not breed or nest in the Carolinas as do Herring and Laughing Gulls. Herring and Laughing Gull nesting colonies often occur in close proximity to one another; the majority of colonies are located on man-made dredge-spoil islands. The nests are located on the ground.

HERONS

pictures 13, 14, 15

Herons are large birds, with long legs, necks and bills. Because herons are shy and reclusive, it is often difficult to get a close look at them. Any effort spent heron-watching is worthwhile, though, as they are fascinating to observe.

Herons feed by wading in shallow water, seeking aquatic animals. Fish provide the bulk of their diet. Sometimes, herons catch fairly large fish and exhibit snake-like ability in swallowing them whole.

The neck of a heron is easily seen when the birds are wading — then, the neck assumes an S-shaped curve. Fifteen to seventeen vertebrae are present in herons' long necks (compared to seven vertebrae in giraffes, man, mice, and almost all other mammals).

The calls of herons are hoarse croaks. If disturbed while feeding, herons are especially prone to voice these croaks as they fly away.

Herons grow areas of specialized powder-down feathers. These feathers fray at the tips, producing a fine powder which is worked into the rest of the birds' feathers. The powder combines with oil and dirt. Herons comb the powder/oil/dirt mixture from their plumage using the nail of their middle toe. After combing, oil from preen glands is applied to the feathers for waterproofing.

The Great Blue Heron is the largest and most majestic of the herons; it stands up to four feet tall. The Great Blue's plumage is blue-gray on the body and white on the head. The large beak is yellow.

When feeding, a Great Blue Heron may stand still as a statue, patiently waiting for fish to snap up with its beak. Or, the bird may wade slowly through the shallows, stirring up animals with its feet.

In flight, the Great Blue Heron exhibits slow, regular beats of its huge wings (up to seven-foot wingspan). The bird flies with its head drawn back to its body — the long neck is not seen in flight. And, believe it or not, this huge bird both mates and nests in trees! Nesting colonies are typically located in swamp forests (not on estuarine or barrier islands like many other coastal birds).

A species sometimes confused with the Great Blue Heron is the Tricolored (Louisiana) Heron. The Tricolored is only half as big, reaching two feet tall. Also, its color pattern is different: the head and body are dark, the underparts white. The Tricolored behaves differently from other herons, too; it wades into deeper water, often up to its abdomen.

Several smaller herons are seen along the Carolina coast. Among these are the Little Blue Heron, the Green-backed Heron, and two species of night herons.

MALLARD DUCK
picture 18

Mallard Ducks are common in sounds, estuaries, and salt marshes of the Carolinas. Male Mallards are easily recognized by their green head, set off by a white neck ring.

Ducks, in general, are aquatic birds with several unique characteristics: flattened bills with tooth-like edges that serve as strainers, long necks, webbed feet, and bodies well-insulated with down.

Mallards are surface-feeding ducks (they rarely dive). To feed, they bob forward, putting their head under the surface, keeping their back end above the water. Mallards eat a largely vegetarian diet, though they consume some insects, small fish, and mollusks.

Mallards fly vigorously. They take off from the water with a bursting upward leap, nearly vertical. In flight, both the male and female flash a bright blue patch of wing feathers, called the speculum. The speculum is located on the back edge of the wing; the blue color is bordered in front and back with white.

Aside from the speculum, the plumage of the male and female Mallard is dramatically different. The male is distinctive, with a rust-colored breast, green head, and white neck band. The female is a mottled, nondescript tan-brown. The female possesses the stronger voice, though, sounding loud quacks; the male makes soft, reedy notes.

Mallard nests consist of depressions in the ground, often located in or near marshes. A natural plant cover typically hides the nest from predators. Females lay five to twelve eggs. The young hatch covered with down; they are capable of swimming and walking a few hours after hatching.

Common white domesticated ducks, or ducks with varying mixtures of the wild Mallard and white plumages, can be seen mingling with groups of Mallards. This is not surprising, as Mallards are the ancestors of common white domestic ducks.

OSPREY
pictures 16, 17

The Osprey, or "Fish Hawk," is one of the most spectacular birds of the seashore. Although relatively uncommon, an Osprey's appearance and behavior are conspicuous, making the bird easy to spot. Anyone lucky enough to observe these birds is captivated by their behavior.

An Osprey is a fairly large bird, with a wingspan of five feet; a characteristic crook in its long wings and a black "wrist" mark distinguish this species even at long distances. The plumage of an Osprey is dark above and white below; the white head is marked by a wide, dark stripe running through the eye.

In behavior, the Osprey is distinctive as well. Its wingbeats are slow and deep, and it flaps more than it sails. **Hovering over water**, at a height of 25 to 150 feet, is characteristic.

When an Osprey spots a fish beneath the surface, the bird suddenly folds its wings and dives toward the water. Nearing the surface, the Osprey spreads its wings to slow down and puts its feet down to grasp the fish with its talons. The bird sometimes completely submerges in an attempt to seize a fish. As the Osprey rises from the water, the bird shakes the water from its plumage, much as a dog shakes water from its fur.

If the hunt is successful, the Osprey flies off, a flapping fish secure in its talons. The Osprey carries the fish head first, presumedly to decrease wind resistance. The bird takes the fish to a favorite feeding perch or returns to feed young birds at its nest.

This behavior (diving for live fish at or just below the surface) is the only method an Osprey uses to capture food. Unlike the Bald Eagle, an Osprey does not scavenge on dead fish.

The eyesight of an Osprey is very keen, which enables it to spot fish from a hundred or more feet above water. Also, rough pads on the soles of its feet help the bird carry large, slippery fish.

Sometimes an Osprey seizes a fish too large to lift out of the water, and it must abandon the fish. Rarely, an Osprey is apparently unable or unwilling to release its hold on a large fish: A dead fish will be found washed ashore, a drowned osprey still clutching its back. Occasionally, an Osprey is robbed of its fish by a group of gulls or a solitary eagle.

The "Fish Hawk" Osprey, expert fisherbird, captures a fish only about one in ten dives. Nine of ten dives, an Osprey comes up empty-taloned. Perhaps fishermen should take heart from the Osprey's success ratio and be glad if they are successful more than ten percent of their fishing trips.

The large nest of an Osprey consists of great masses of sticks (*picture 17*). The nests are often visible in the tops of large trees adjacent to water or on navigational markers in waterways and channels. Each year, a pair of Ospreys returns to the same nest, adding more sticks and branches; the nest grows larger in size, sometimes reaching 1,000 or even 1,500 pounds! Occasionally, a nest collapses from the sheer weight.

Ospreys can live into their twenties, and a pair normally mates for life. The yearly courtship ritual of Ospreys is a thrilling sight. The male bird dives swiftly downward from great heights; he approaches the female and offers her a fish, his pre-mating gift.

Ospreys, like other birds of prey, were decimated by widespread use of DDT and other insecticides. These toxins result in thin, fragile eggshells, with resultant low survival rates. Since these pesticides have been banned in the U.S., Ospreys are making a comeback.

OYSTERCATCHER
picture 19

The American Oystercatcher is eye-catching, mainly because of its large, bright-red bill. The spectacular "red cigar" beak gives the bird a character all its own.

The Oystercatcher is a heavy-bodied bird, with white undersides, black head and back. Upon taking flight, the Oystercatcher flashes a chevron: a white wingstripe on its black wings. Perhaps a simpler description of this bird is "the bird with a big red nose, wearing a tuxedo."

The Oystercatcher is larger in size than many shorebirds. Upon closer inspection, it has pink legs and an orange ring around each eye.

The red bill of the Oystercatcher is not only spectacular in appearance — the bill is specially adapted for the Oystercatcher's feeding habits. The bill is used in the behavior which gives the bird its name. Oysters or other mollusks are sought on a falling tide. Upon finding an oyster, an Oystercatcher stabs its beak inside the shell. Using the bill as a chisel, it snips the oyster's adductor muscle, which holds the shellfish closed. The bird then removes the oyster from the shell and eats it.

With its unique oystering method, an Oystercatcher can open and consume the largest oysters. Most of the oysters eaten by Oystercatchers are small specimens not commercially valuable.

In addition to clams, oysters, and other bivalves, the Oystercatcher eats other small seashore creatures. Its bill enables the Oystercatcher to eat sea urchins by turning them upside down and picking out the insides (without even breaking the shell). An Oystercatcher also uses its bill to probe the sand for small animals. Fiddlers and other small crabs, snails, shrimp, and marine worms make up part of the bird's diet.

The Oystercatcher is found on sandy beaches and coastal mudflats, but it is not a common sight. The bird prefers wilder coastal areas, free of human presence. Most often, Oystercatchers gather in small groups, frequently in pairs or quartets. Oystercatchers do not often mingle with other species of shorebirds.

Oystercatchers are not only strong fliers, they are also rapid runners. When approached, the birds utter sharp cries of alarm as they take flight.

Unlike many shorebirds in the Carolinas, Oystercatchers are permanent residents: They do not migrate to nest. Isolated beaches and offshore islands are nesting sights of Oystercatchers. The nests are shallow hollows located on bare sandy areas behind frontal dunes. The nests typically contain one to three eggs; the eggs are gray with irregular dark splotches.

Oystercatchers are usually four years old before they mate. They have a lifespan of up to 20 years.

16

RUDDY TURNSTONE
picture 20

The Ruddy Turnstone is a shorebird common to the Carolina coast. This species is most often seen in the surf zone of ocean beaches. The few rocky areas on the Carolina coast (natural or man-made jetties) also attract these birds.

The distinctive marking of the Turnstone is its black vest. Orange legs and a black-and-white facial mask also help identify the Ruddy. The Ruddy has been called the "Calico Bird," with its brown, black, and white patches on its wings, rump, and tail. All these markings are bright and obvious in the breeding season, duller in the winter.

The bill of the Turnstone is also distinctive: thick at the base, tapering to a pointed tip, and slightly upturned at the end. The beak is black in color.

A Ruddy uses its beak to dig holes in the sand to look for crustaceans. The bird's last name, Turnstone, refers to another feeding method: A Turnstone will turn over shells, stones, sticks, and seaweed with its beak, looking for beach fleas, worms, small crabs, and mollusks. On occasion, a Turnstone opens a mollusk shell by hammering the shell with its beak.

One or two Turnstones are often seen mingling with Sanderlings and Willets, birds present in greater numbers in the surf zone. Ruddys are intermediate in size between these two species, reaching about seven inches in length.

In late May, Ruddy Turnstones make a long flight back to their breeding/nesting grounds in the Arctic.

SANDERLING
picture 21

The Sanderling is a small, animated bird found in small flocks on sandy ocean beaches.

Weighing just two to three ounces, the Sanderling is one of the smaller shorebirds. Sanderlings are gray on top and white below; the beak and legs are black. Summer plumage is more rust-colored than gray.

Typically, Sanderlings skitter back and forth, running up the beach with an incoming wave, then back down as the wave recedes. Their tiny black legs churn rapidly as they scurry to feed on food exposed by the waves. With probing beaks, Sanderlings search the sand for small animals such as Mole Crabs.

When approached on the beach, a flock of Sanderlings will flee as a group; each bird flashes a distinct white wing stripe upon taking flight. The birds fly up or down the beach, parallel to the water's edge, before landing to resume feeding.

These tiny birds were once shot in great numbers for human food, decreasing their population. Now, they are again abundant, much to the delight and entertainment of beachcombers.

Sanderlings, along with Mole Crabs and Coquina Clams, are members of the "swash community." The swash zone is the intertidal area between the low and high tide marks on the beach. The species adapted to this area are few, but the species present are often found in great numbers.

Many shorebirds feed in the marsh at low tide and feed on the beach at high tide, when the marsh is flooded. The Sanderling is an exception: It is primarily a beach feeder.

Like many other shorebirds of the Carolinas, Sanderlings do not breed here. Like Ruddy Turnstones, they breed in the Arctic and subarctic regions.

TERNS
pictures 10, 11, 12

Terns are often confused with their close relatives, the gulls. Terns are more slender (diagram 1) and more agile in flight than gulls. In addition, terns have straight bills and forked tails (gulls typically have hooked bills and squared tails). The aerobatics (aerial acrobatics) and forked tails of terns have earned them the nickname "sea swallows."

Diagram 1
Terns are slender birds, with forked tails and straight bills. Gulls have larger bodies, squared tails, and hooked bills.

Terns also are more specialized than gulls in behavior and feeding habits. They do not scavenge for food but feed almost exclusively on live fish.

Watching terns feed is a delight. Typically, a tern hovers over the water when hunting. When it spies a fish, it suddenly folds its wings and dives headfirst toward the surface. The bird hits the water like a dart, making a small splash. Sometimes the tern completely submerges, going several feet under water to capture its prey. If successful, the tern emerges with a small fish held crosswise in its beak. The bird typically swallows the fish while flying or, if nesting, takes the fish to its offspring.

Adult terns feed their offspring differently from gulls. Parent terns carry tiny fish in their beaks back to the nest and the food is thrust into the young birds' gullets. Gulls simply regurgitate already-swallowed food onto the ground; young gulls scoop it up with their beaks.

A dozen or more tern species are seen on the Carolina coast. In general, terns are white birds with some sort of black cap. Perhaps it is enough to simply identify a bird as a tern and enjoy its behavior. Four relatively common species of terns occur here, though, that can be differentiated fairly easily. Commonly seen terns include the Least, Common, Royal, and Caspian.

The LEAST TERN is easily distinguished by its **small size**, being noticeably smaller than other local terns. Besides its small size, the Least is identified by a yellow bill, yellow legs, and broad tail. The black cap of the Least Tern is highlighted by the bird's white forehead.

A medium-sized bird, the COMMON TERN has a black-tipped, red-orange bill, deeply forked tail, and red feet. It is the most common U.S. tern.

The ROYAL TERN is one of the largest terns. In addition to its thick body, the Royal is characterized by a shaggy black crest on its head, a thick **orange bill**, and a noticeably forked tail.

Although similar in size and appearance to the Royal Tern, the CASPIAN TERN is distinguished from the Royal by its **blood-red bill**. Also, the Caspian's tail is only slightly forked, and it behaves more like a gull (for example, it often alights on water).

Least, Common, Royal, and Caspian Terns nest in the Carolinas. Like most all tern species, these birds nest in colonies. Colonies are located near ocean beaches or on estuarine islands. Nests consist of small depressions dug in the sand (terns are ground nesters).

If a nesting colony is approached by a potential predator (such as man), the adult birds become greatly agitated. Flying overhead, they swoop toward the head of the intruder, stopping just short of colliding; at the same time, the terns sound piercing cries and often defecate. The threatening attacks often persuade the intruder to retreat from the nesting site. Prompt withdrawal by the intruder is essential, as tern eggs or young may die if exposed to either hot or cold temperatures for long.

Terns are among the animals which have been most affected by man's actions (and continue to be affected).

The Least Tern was hunted to near-extinction during the late 1800's. This travesty resulted from fashion designers using whole terns to decorate women's hats. The Least Tern was the species most affected by this unthinking action, as it nests on less remote beaches more accessible to man. Least Terns were literally slaughtered by the thousands at their nesting sites. In this instance, man could see that this direct action was harmful. Laws were enacted to protect terns and other shorebirds before they joined the Passenger Pigeon in the "Hall of Extinction."

The Common Tern population was also decimated by "hat hunters." Common Terns are still being affected by more subtle human influences. As coastal development increases, trash dumps and other areas where Herring Gulls scavenge proliferate; this increased food supply results in an increasing Herring Gull population. Herring Gulls prey on the young and eggs of small ground-nesting birds (such as Common Terns). Thus, as a result of development, the population of Common Terns has decreased. In this instance, indirect actions of man have affected terns.

Probably the biggest adverse impact tern populations face is loss of nesting habitat. As beachfront development grows, available tern nesting sites decrease. All-terrain vehicle traffic and even foot traffic disturbs nesting sites.

Fortunately, man's growing coastal presence has also had a positive effect upon tern populations. When dredging is done to clear river channels, inlets, or waterways, excess sand is deposited in huge piles; dredge-spoil islands are thus created. Terns prefer uninhabited, sandy, water-adjacent areas for nesting sites, so they have proliferated on these man-made islands.

WHITE IBIS

picture 22

The White Ibis is a secretive bird, generally avoiding areas of human habitation. Coastal residents visiting unspoiled, natural locations are more likely to see the White Ibis.

The appearance of the White Ibis is spectacular. The bird's plumage is bright white. The Ibis's bill is unique: It is long, downcurved, and reddish. An area of facial skin behind the bill is also red. Black wing tips highlight the white plumage; the black markings are seen when the bird flies and are not usually visible at rest. The bird's legs and bill are bright red during the breeding season, pinkish-gray at other times.

A White Ibis stands about two feet tall; the wingspan measures up to three feet. Typical of wading birds, the White Ibis has long legs, neck, and bill. The area of red facial skin is bare of feathers.

The distinctive downcurved, red bill is used in feeding: The bill sweeps the water for animals or probes the mud for Fiddler Crabs, snails, worms, and insects. The male Ibis's bill is several inches longer than the female's.

Immature Ibises are a mottled brown. The young birds have a white belly and rump; the white rump is conspicuous when a young bird flies away from an observer. The white markings, along with the downcurved red bill, distinguish even young Ibises from other species.

The calls of the White Ibis are low, harsh grunts.

Ibises congregate in flocks, whether feeding on tidal flats or flying. In flight, Ibises can be distinguished from other wading birds by their outstretched necks (herons and egrets fly with their neck curved in an S shape). Flocks of Ibises are often seen high overhead, forming a long line or V-formation. The birds alternate between flapping and gliding; the wingbeats are rapid.

Like herons and egrets, White Ibises nest in large colonies; the colonies are located in trees and shrubs near water. The stick nests are often crowded together, up to 70 nests per tree.

Ibis parents feed their young regurgitated fish. If a nesting site is disturbed, immature birds may fall from the nest. The young birds sometimes attempt to clamber back up the tree to safety, but most often they succumb.

Ibises are relatively recent inhabitants of the Carolina coast. Fifty years ago, White Ibises resided in Florida; since then, the birds have gradually expanded their range north to include both South and North Carolina.

WILLET

picture 23

The Willet is a member of the shorebird family, birds that frequent beaches, sounds, and tidal mud flats. The numerous species of shorebirds are often difficult to tell apart. The Willet, though, is fairly easy to identify; it is also one of the most common shorebirds.

A fairly large bird, the Willet stands about a foot tall. At first glance, the Willet is nondescript, gray in the winter and brown in the summer. When approached, however, the Willet flies off, signalling its identity. A chevron pattern, a white stripe bordered by black, is flashed on the wings; this pattern is diagnostic for the Willet. Also, the bird often utters several piercing cries as it flies off.

Willets are most commonly seen in the surf zone of ocean beaches (where waves roll in). Here, they wander up and down the beach, probing with long bills for Mole Crabs, worms, and other small animals. Willets often mingle with Sanderlings on the beach, and the contrast in size between the two species is remarkable.

Willets nest in the Carolinas. The nests are located in secondary dunes behind the beach, or in grassy areas near marshes. The nests consist of grass-lined hollows in the ground. The nests are typically sheltered and hidden by surrounding clumps of grass. One to four green-gray eggs, speckled with black, are laid.

If humans approach a nesting area, Willets become very agitated. The adult birds fly back and forth over the area, screaming cries of alarm. At times, they dive close to intruders, feigning attack.

Photo by Richard E. Bird, M.D.

1. Black Skimmer (page 6)

Photo by Richard E. Bird, M.D.

2. Black Skimmer (page 6)

3. Brown Pelican (page 7)

4. Double-crested Cormorant (page 9)

5. Great Egret (page 10)

6. Snowy Egret (page 10)

7. Laughing Gull (page 11)

8. Ring-billed Gull (page 11)

9. Herring Gulls, *adult and immature* (page 11)

10. Least Tern (page 18)

Photo by Richard E. Bird, M.D.

11. Common Tern (page 18)

Photo by Richard E. Bird, M.D.

12. Royal Tern (page 18)

13. Great Blue Heron (page 13)

14. Tricolored Heron (page 13)

15. Green-backed Heron (page 13)

16. Osprey (page 14)

17. Ospreys *on nest* (page 14)

18. Mallard Ducks, *male and two females* (page 14)

19. Oystercatcher (page 16)

Photo by Bob Slaughter

20. Ruddy Turnstone (page 17)

Photo by Bob Slaughter

21. Sanderling (page 17)

22. White Ibis (page 20)

23. Willet (page 21)

CRABS AND
OTHER CRUSTACEANS

Everyone knows what a crab is — a hard-shelled animal with pincers. But scientists use the terms crab, "true crab," and crustacean to mean different things. And Horseshoe Crabs are classified apart, as neither crabs nor crustaceans. The organization of crab-like animals into related groups is confusing, but can be understood as follows (diagram 2):

Crabs and crustaceans belong to the phylum Arthropoda. Arthropods are the most numerous and widespread group of animals on earth, numbering nearly a million species. Seventy-five percent of all animals are arthropods. They occupy almost every environmental niche in the world.

Arthropods are invertebrate animals (no backbone), with segmented bodies, jointed legs, and a hard exoskeleton (outer shell). Land arthropods include insects, spiders, mites, scorpions, millipedes, and centipedes. Marine arthropods include the Horseshoe Crab, sea spiders and crustaceans.

The Horseshoe Crab is unique enough to be classified by itself. Technically, it is neither crab nor crustacean.

Sea spiders are tiny (1/16 to 1/2 inch) animals that resemble land spiders. Though common, sea spiders are inconspicuous, blending into heavy growth of plants and animals on rocks and pilings.

Crustaceans include barnacles, Mole Crabs, Hermit Crabs, shrimps, lobsters, and "true crabs." Barnacles, though they resemble mollusks, are actually sessile crustaceans. Mole Crabs, Hermit Crabs, shrimp, and lobster are classified separately from "true crabs" by subtle differences in body form and leg location. "True crabs" include species such as Blue, Fiddler, Ghost, Marsh, Oyster, and Stone Crabs. "True crabs" are short-tailed crustaceans (tail folded under the thorax), with the front pair of feet modified into pincers.

If the classification of crabs and crustaceans is still confusing, do not

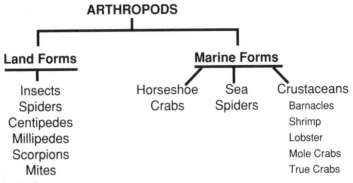

ARTHROPODS

Land Forms

Insects
Spiders
Centipedes
Millipedes
Scorpions
Mites

Marine Forms

Horseshoe
Crabs

Sea
Spiders

Crustaceans

Barnacles
Shrimp
Lobster
Mole Crabs
True Crabs

Diagram 2
Classification of crab-like animals. Crustaceans are the marine equivalent of insects, spiders, scorpions, et al.

despair: Think of crustaceans as creatures occupying marine niches corresponding to terrestrial niches of their land relatives; in other words, crustaceans are the marine equivalent of insects, spiders, scorpions, et al. Marine arthropods grow bigger because water helps support the weight of their shell; land arthropods are limited in size by the weight of their exoskeleton.

Molting is a process common to crustaceans (and many land arthropods, too). To grow in size, a crustacean periodically sheds its external shell. A new shell is hardened in a few days time; a newly-molted crustacean is vulnerable to predators until its shell is hard.

Most crustaceans undergo metamorphosis during their early development. Metamorphosis is the distinct change in body form an animal undergoes developing from an embryo to an adult. Early forms often do not resemble adult animals (diagram 3).

Amazingly, crustaceans are able to break off one or more legs as an escape mechanism. If a predator grabs hold of a crab's leg, the predator

Diagram 3
Changes in body form during metamorphosis of a crab.

may pull the leg off, or the crab may break off its own leg and flee. This process, called autotomy, sacrifices a limb to save the crab's life. The limb breaks off at a specific joint specially adapted not to bleed if the limb is severed. The crab (or other crustacean) regrows the lost limb at later molts, though it may take three to four molts for the limb to attain full size.

While most crabs swim poorly, a few species, such as the Blue Crab, swim quite well. The Blue Crab and other swimming crabs have the ends of the last pair of legs modified into wide, flat paddles.

The crabs and crustaceans of the Carolina coast, like their counterparts world-wide, are numerous and successful. Yet, our local "insects of the sea" possess their own unique and interesting characteristics. The following sections focus on the most common local crabs and crustaceans.

BLUE CRAB
pictures 24, 25

The Blue Crab is the common edible crab of the Atlantic coast. Delicious white meat makes it the object of amateur and professional crabbers alike.

The Blue Crab is actually olive-green on most of its body; its name stems from blue coloration on its claws and legs. The tips of the crab's claws and body spines are usually red, while its underside is white.

Like all true crabs, the Blue Crab has five pairs of legs. The first pair of legs is modified into pincers. The next three pairs are walking legs, while the last pair is modified into paddle-like structures for swimming.

Eyes on the ends of movable stalks give the crab two advantages: 1) 360-degree vision, and 2) the ability to retract the eyes into grooves on its shell when danger threatens.

The male Blue Crab grows a little larger than the female and has a sharply-pointed apron on the bottom of his shell (diagram 4, *picture 25*). The female has a rounded apron on her underside. An easy way to visualize the difference: The male's apron resembles the Washington Monument, the female's apron resembles the Capitol Dome. The female crab often carries a mass of orange eggs on her underside; she is said to be "in sponge," as the egg mass resembles a sponge. Juvenile females exhibit a triangular apron.

The red coloration on the claw tips is much more prominent on the female, as well. The male has red only on the extreme tips of his claws,

Diagram 4
The gender of a Blue Crab can be determined by looking at the crab's underside.

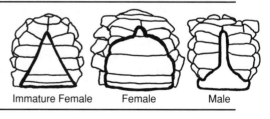

Immature Female   Female   Male

while the female has much more red on her claws, easily seen at a glance. Remember this difference by thinking of the female "painting" her nails (claws) a bright red, like a human female painting her nails.

The points, spines, and claws of the Blue Crab give it a menacing appearance. The crab's powerful claws can, in fact, inflict a painful wound. A Blue Crab can be picked up safely, though, by grasping it at the rear of its body, between the last pair of legs; held there, the crab cannot pinch one's fingers.

The male Blue Crab spends its adult life in the brackish water of sounds and estuaries. The female resides there until her eggs are ready to hatch. She then travels out an inlet to the open ocean and releases her eggs.

Crab hatchlings begin life as zooplankton in the open ocean. Crab larvae undergo seven or eight changes in body shape before attaining adult form; the adult-shaped crab that results is the size of a pinhead. The tiny crab then rides ocean currents back into sounds and estuaries.

The young Blue Crab grows rapidly, reaching one to two inches in length by the time it buries itself in a muddy bottom for its first winter. The crab grows to adult size in estuaries, undergoing 20 or more molts before it is full-grown. On the average, only a few of the original two million-or-so eggs laid by a single female reach adulthood.

Molting is the process which enables a crab to enlarge its soft inner body yet maintain its dead, non-growing, outside shell (exoskeleton). When a crab grows to the point it must shed its shell, the crab is known as a "peeler." During the 48 hours after a crab sheds, it is a "softshell" crab; the crab is defenseless until its new shell hardens.

Interestingly, a female crab can mate only after molting. In fact, she must mate within minutes after she molts for the last time in her life. To assure copulation in this narrow time frame, a male crab "cradles" a female crab, carrying her gently underneath him for two to three days prior to molting. Although mating is once-in-a-lifetime for a female, it lasts six to twelve hours. After mating, the male crab continues to cradle the female, carrying her two to three more days. The female crab is thus protected by the male until her shell hardens.

The adaptability of the Blue Crab is amazing. It survives in salinities varying from the open ocean to fresh water. If a leg is lost in a fight, a Blue Crab is able to grow a new one. A Blue Crab can crawl across the bottom, swim rapidly, or even burrow into sandy bottom for protection. While often scavenging on dead animals, the Blue Crab is also a capable predator, capturing small fish, shrimp, and crabs.

One thing which the Blue Crab does not adapt to is man's pollution; it disappears from waters that become heavily polluted.

Blue Crabs are usually eaten in the "hardshell" form; the crabs are steamed and the meat is picked from the claws and body. Blue Crabs can also be eaten in the "softshell" form; recently-molted crabs are cleaned, then fried and eaten whole.

Man is not the only animal to seek Blue Crabs for food; they are also eaten by gulls, herons, octopuses, and numerous species of fish.

FIDDLER CRAB
picture 26

Groups of Fiddler Crabs congregate in salt marshes and tidal flats. When approached, they scurry away en masse, often making a noticeable rustling.

The appearance of male Fiddlers is unmistakable: The crabs have an oversized claw on one side (diagram 5), which they wave to defend territory and attract mates.

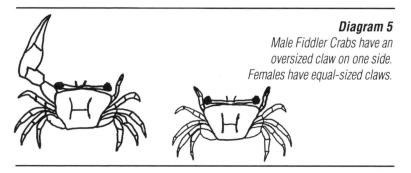

Diagram 5
Male Fiddler Crabs have an oversized claw on one side. Females have equal-sized claws.

The holes of Fiddler Crab burrows are easily spotted in the marsh. They are dime-sized openings in the muddy soil, with stacks of pellets nearby.

Fiddlers burrow by scraping sand and mud into pellets, then carrying the pellets out of the burrow and depositing them on the marsh surface; after the crabs drop the pellets, they scurry back to their holes. Fiddler burrows, one to two feet in depth, enable the crabs to escape predators. The burrows serve the marsh as well — they ventilate the marsh mud at low tide and irrigate it at high tide.

During high tide, Fiddlers place a mud plug in their burrow tunnels, staying "low and dry" until the tide recedes. In the winter, Fiddlers disappear into their burrows for a type of hibernation. With the arrival of warm weather, they once again march on the marsh.

Almost exclusively herbivorous (vegetarian), Fiddler Crabs feed on the abundant algae in their habitat. Like all true crabs, Fiddlers' first pair of legs is modified into pincers. In Fiddlers, these pincers are spoonlike, enabling them to scrape algae. Female crabs feed by rapidly alternating right and left claws, like children stuffing candy into their mouths as fast as they can. Males eat with just one claw since their other oversized claw is adapted for territorial defense and courtship behavior.

Using their mouth parts, Fiddlers separate algae from mud and sand. The sand and mud are discarded before the algae is ingested. This method of eating contrasts with that of many worms: The worms ingest sand and mud along with their food, later excreting the undigested sand and mud in their waste.

Fiddler Crabs, along with Ghost Crabs, are in the family Ocypodidae, meaning "swift-footed." Any sudden movement sends them scrambling for cover. One must be very quick to catch Fiddlers by hand or net before they disappear into their holes. Fiddler crabs are sought because they make good fish bait; Sheepshead, especially, are prone to bite a hook baited with a Fiddler Crab.

Fiddlers are named for the appearance and behavior of the males; when male crabs wave their large claw back and forth, they resemble base fiddle players. Large numbers of males often wave their kingsized claws at the same time; this behavior has been termed the "fiddler fiddle" or "marshland discomania."

Animals that prey on Fiddler Crabs include shorebirds, raccoons, terrapins, fish, and larger crabs.

GHOST CRAB
picture 27

Ghost Crabs inhabit the dry upper area of ocean beaches. They are easily noticed when they scurry back and forth on the sand — when still, they blend so well with their environment that they are hard to see.

The square body of the Ghost Crab is only 1.5 to 2 inches wide, but long legs make the crab look larger. The top of the crab is off-white to tan, about the color of the sand it inhabits; the underside is whiter. The Ghost Crab's pincers are white, sometimes tinted with lavender. "Periscope" eyes are mounted on the ends of stalks, which rotate to provide 360-degree vision. A Ghost Crab can protect its eyes by retracting them into grooves on the front of its shell.

Although much more active at night, Ghost Crabs are seen during the day as well. Most often, the beachcomber will catch just a glimpse of a Ghost Crab scampering across the beach to disappear into its hole. The crab can run sideways, forward, or backward on its spindly legs. If one sits quietly a few minutes near the hole, the crab will reappear and venture forth again.

The burrow holes of the Ghost Crab are as large as three inches in diameter; they are located in the dry upper portion of the beach. The tunnel leading to the crab's burrow may go down four feet in the sand. Ghost crabs remain dormant in their burrows during the winter months.

Even though the Ghost Crab lives in the desert-like habitat of the upper beach zone, it remains a marine animal. Several times a day, the crab must return to the ocean shallows to wet its gills. The Ghost Crab is apparently in the midst of an evolutionary change; it is evolving from a past existence as a sea animal to a future as a dry-land animal.

Unlike many of its crab relatives, the Ghost Crab does not possess a thick protective shell, nor are its pinching claws very powerful. A Ghost Crab does, however, possess the attributes of protective coloration, swift locomotion, and rapid burrowing ability. These factors adapt it well to its environment.

The Ghost Crab seeks more live prey, and is less a scavenger, than other crabs. A Ghost Crab preys on Beach Fleas, Mole Crabs, Coquina Clams, sea turtle hatchlings, and other small animals; dead flesh and beach debris are also eaten. Ghost Crabs are, in turn, eaten by animals such as gulls and raccoons.

Humans do not usually eat Ghost Crabs, at least in the Carolinas; Ghost Crabs are eaten on some Caribbean islands.

The female Ghost Crab deposits her eggs directly into the ocean (more evidence of an ocean-based existence for Ghost Crab ancestors). Ghost Crab larvae become part of the free-floating zooplankton and undergo several life-form changes while developing. The mature crab emerges from the ocean to spend its life on land (except for its gill-wetting dashes).

Ghost Crabs are common on undisturbed beaches. They are scarce on beaches used heavily by people. In fact, Ghost Crabs are typically absent from resort areas using machines to clean their beaches.

HERMIT CRAB
picture 28

Interestingly, the Hermit Crab resides not in a shell of its own making, but in a shell "borrowed" from another animal. A Hermit Crab most often occupies the shell of an already-dead gastropod (snail-like animal).

The Hermit Crab needs a shell to protect its softer rear parts, for only the Hermit Crab's head and claws are calcified. The last two pairs of the crab's legs are modified to hold the crab inside its adopted shell. In fact, the crab holds so tightly that it will be pulled apart if attempts are made to forcibly pull it out.

As a Hermit Crab grows and molts, its shell must be discarded for a larger one. Normally, the crab locates an empty shell to use. Rarely, a crab will fight another Hermit Crab to evict it from its shell, stealing the shell to use.

When threatened, a Hermit Crab withdraws into its shell, closing off the opening with its hard claws. Like Fiddler Crabs, Hermit Crabs have un-equal claws (one side is larger); unlike Fiddlers, both sexes of Hermit Crabs have unequal claws. The left claw of hermit crabs is smaller than the right, perhaps because it is better able to seal the opening to its shell.

Shallow protected waters are the habitat of the Hermit Crab. Aquatic Hermit Crabs can survive out of water for short periods of time. The aquatic species found in Carolina waters are not like other species of Hermit Crabs (sold in pet stores) that are land-oriented, air-breathing animals.

Animals such as sea anemones, barnacles, and hydroids sometimes live on the shells of Hermit Crabs. These animals exhibit a symbiotic relationship with the Hermit Crab: They live in close association, to the benefit of both animals. For example, the presence of an anemone may protect the Hermit Crab from predators, while the anemone gathers scraps of food when the Hermit Crab eats.

Hermit Crabs are mainly scavengers, eating dead animals and debris. At times, though, they are carnivorous, eating small live animals. Hermit Crabs may even eat their own kind when a fellow Hermit is found outside its shell (such as when a crab changes from one shell to another). The Hermit Crab, in turn, is eaten by many kinds of fish and shorebirds.

For the gastronomically brave, Hermit Crabs are edible. They are cooked and eaten in the same manner as common edible crabs.

HORSESHOE CRAB

picture 29

The Horseshoe Crab is aptly called a "living fossil," as it is one of the oldest known living species of animals; these animals have lived in the oceans for more than 600 million years — since before dinosaurs roamed the earth!

The Horseshoe Crab is not a "true" crab, nor is it a crustacean; the Horseshoe Crab is in a separate class by itself. The closest living relatives of the Horseshoe Crab are spiders.

Although menacing in appearance, a Horseshoe Crab is quite harmless. Limulus, as it is also known (from an older scientific name), can be safely picked up and examined in detail.

A Horseshoe Crab resembles a flattened helmet, trailing a spiked tail (diagram 6). On its underside, the front part of its shell has the shape of a horseshoe; the central part is all legs, with five pairs of walking legs. The mouth of the animal is located between the last three pairs of legs. The unique breathing apparatus of the Horseshoe Crab, six pairs of book gills, is behind the legs.

The appendages of the Horseshoe Crab have unusual functions. The spiked tail is used as a lever to right the animal if it is turned on its back by surf or currents. The legs provide locomotion and also grind food eaten by the animal. As a Horseshoe Crab walks, spines on the upper joint of each leg chew its food, much like teeth. The food is then passed backward through the legs into the mouth. As a matter of fact, the Horseshoe Crab is

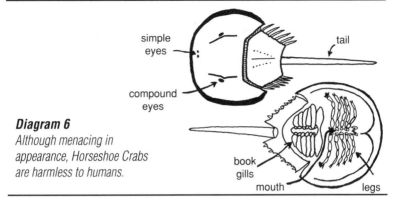

simple
eyes

tail

compound
eyes

Diagram 6
*Although menacing in
appearance, Horseshoe Crabs
are harmless to humans.*

book
gills

mouth

legs

unable to eat except when walking.

The book gills of the crab can breathe both water and air. There are two pairs of eyes, one pair fairly large, and another smaller pair farther forward. The eyes are fixed in the shell, unlike eyes of true crabs, which are placed on the ends of stalks.

The Horseshoe Crab ranges from the shallows of the surf to 75 feet deep. It plows slowly through bottom sand and mud, preying on mollusks, crustaceans, worms, and other small animals. A Horseshoe Crab can be quite destructive to clam beds.

Most often, Horseshoe Crabs are observed when they crawl on shore to breed. From spring to early summer, Horseshoe Crabs perform their breeding ritual: A female crab crawls out of the surf; clinging to her are one or more males. The female makes a small hollow in the sand, just below the mean high-tide line, and deposits thousands of eggs. The males deposit sperm on the eggs, and the eggs are covered with sand. A female may nest ten times each season, laying a total of more than 20,000 eggs.

Horseshoe Crab eggs are eaten by birds, crabs, and other animals of the surf area. Surviving eggs hatch in July and August, and quarter-sized, tailless, miniature replicas of adults emerge. The young Horseshoe Crabs grow in shallow water. After several molts (the Horseshoe Crab, too, sheds its skin to grow), adult size is attained. The crabs take nine to eleven years to mature sexually, when they migrate back to their home beaches to breed.

Adult Horseshoe Crabs often serve as home and transportation for other animals: Barnacles, tube worms, and slipper shells sometimes make their homes on the Horseshoe Crab's shell. Inch-long, white-to-tan flatworms live on the crab's book gills.

The blood of a Horseshoe Crab turns blue, not red, when exposed to air. The blood is distinctive, containing copper instead of iron. Also, Horseshoe Crab blood cells react strongly when exposed to some bacteria. As a result of these unique properties, Horseshoe Crab blood is used extensively in medical research; current studies attempt to detect serious bacterial infections (such as meningitis) in man. Horseshoe Crab blood cells are also used extensively in tests to make certain no impurities exist in medicines and intravenous fluids.

Although Horseshoe Crabs can be eaten, they rarely are. In the past, Horseshoe Crabs were used for fertilizer.

MARSH CRAB

picture 30

The Marsh Crab is small, about one inch across; it is similar in size to the Fiddler Crab.

A distinguishing characteristic of the Marsh Crab is its nearly square carapace (body). Other features include a dark brown or olive color, two black eyes located at the front corners of the shell, long thin legs, and two tiny, purplish claws.

Living up to its name, the main habitat of this crab is the marsh. The burrows of the Marsh Crab are in the upper areas of the marsh, often mixed in with those of Fiddler Crabs. The Marsh Crab is one of few animals that actually feeds on the marsh grass itself; it prefers the older outer leaves of Spartina Grass. Algae and small dead animals are also eaten.

Interestingly, the Marsh Crab is semi-terrestrial. It makes frequent forays from marshes into environments inhabited by man. Anyone who lives adjacent to a marsh is likely to see these tiny crabs, scurrying to hide under rocks or logs. Marsh Crabs seem to possess a friendly, almost endearing nature.

Other common names of the Marsh Crab include Square-backed Crab, Mud Crab, and Purple Marsh Crab. The name Marsh Crab seems to fit it best.

OYSTER CRAB

picture 31

Oyster Crabs are tiny (less than one-half inch) species that live inside the shells of live oysters and other bivalves. Most often, Oyster Crabs are discovered when a shellfish connoisseur opens an oyster to eat the shellfish. Usually, the oyster-eater will go ahead and eat the Oyster Crab as well. After all, if one is willing to eat a slimy, shapeless oyster, what's a little crab to boot?

The shell of Oyster Crabs is white, fragile, and thin — paperlike in quality. The body shape of the crabs is round.

The Oyster Crab is largely commensal with its oyster host, meaning it lives with the oyster and shares its benefits. When the oyster opens its shell to feed, the crab obtains plankton and detritus (small particles of decaying matter) to feed upon. Predators have difficulty getting at the crab, as the shell of the oyster protects it.

The Oyster Crab is not purely commensal, however. At times the Oyster Crab is parasitic, eating the tissue of the oyster and also robbing it of food.

Oyster Crabs and related species live in oysters, scallops, mussels, tube worms, sand dollars, and sea urchins. More than 200 Oyster Crabs have been found in a single oyster at a time!

Young Oyster Crabs enter the siphon system of oysters in late summer. After residing in the mollusk for one year, males leave on a free-swimming "nuptial flight" to find females in other oysters. Males die after mating, while females become soft-shelled and live two to three more years. Males grow up to three-sixteenths inch, females to one-half inch. Due to their small size, Oyster Crabs are also known as Pea Crabs.

STONE CRAB
picture 32

The Stone Crab is easily recognized by its dark, heavy shell, and large claws. Stone Crab claw meat is highly regarded by seafood lovers.

A Stone Crab may grow to five inches wide. Its oval shell is brownish-red with gray spots, tan underneath. The pincers of the Stone Crab are heavy and unequal; the fingers (ends) of the pincers are black (a nickname of the Stone Crab is "black fingers"). The walking legs of the Stone Crab are heavy and hairy.

The unequal claws of the Stone Crab have different functions. The large, blunt-edged claw is used to hold and crush food. The smaller, saw-edged claw is used to pinch, rip, and tear the crab's prey. The powerful claws can crush human fingers if a Stone Crab is handled carelessly. Fortunately, Stone Crabs are slower-moving and less aggressive than Blue Crabs.

The Stone Crab is the largest member of the mud crab family. Unlike the Blue Crab, the Stone Crab does not swim. Adult Stone Crabs are common on rock jetties; they also inhabit deep burrows dug into soft bottom sediments. Young crabs are found in grass and shell bottoms of channels.

Stone Crabs prey on barnacles, as well as small oysters and clams. The heavy claws of Stone Crabs can easily crack the shells of smaller mollusks.

The claw meat of Stone Crabs is considered a delicacy. The harvest of Stone Crabs is regulated in most states. In some states (including South Carolina), only the larger claw of a Stone Crab may be taken; the claw is broken off and the live crab is returned to the water. Like most crustaceans, the Stone Crab is able to regenerate an appendage in two months.

BARNACLES

pictures 34, 35

Almost everyone has seen barnacles; their small volcano-shaped shells cover pilings, rocks, boat bottoms, and seashells. Barnacles must lead pretty boring and humdrum lives, stuck to something, right? Wrong! As a matter of fact, barnacles can be compared to humans: They spend the first part of their lives wandering, before "settling down" to a permanent abode.

The life of a barnacle begins when one barnacle extends a slender sperm tube out from its shell into the shell of an adjacent barnacle. Eggs are fertilized and hatched inside the parent barnacle. The microscopic larvae soon leave the parent barnacle, joining the free-floating zooplankton for several weeks.

After several molts and a metamorphosis, a tiny barnacle settles head-first on a hard surface; glue is secreted from the animal's antenna glands. The barnacle then changes to its adult form (without eyes or sensory appendages). A six-part, cone-shaped, calcium carbonate shell is secreted around the soft body. Six pairs of larval legs become cirri, fan-like structures which rhythmically wave, pulling in water and plankton for the animal to consume. The cirri correspond to walking legs on crabs and lobster.

Although barnacles are hermaphroditic (both sexes in the same animal), reproduction is usually by cross-fertilization. Barnacles easily locate an adjacent barnacle for reproduction, as there may be thousands of barnacles per square meter. It is not unusual to find barnacles crowded on top of older barnacles.

Young barnacles are very selective as to where they attach; a hard surface already colonized by other barnacles is preferred. In addition, barnacles are found on living animals, such as turtles, crabs, whales, and Horseshoe Crabs.

The location of barnacle beds pretty well defines the upper limits of the high tide splash zone, as they must be covered with water twice a day to survive. When the tide falls below the barnacles' level, they retract their cirri and close their shells to avoid drying.

Although barnacles are most visible in shallow areas, they do live in deeper water as well. Some species of barnacles lack shells and live as parasites on crabs, sea stars, coral, sponges, and other animals.

Along the Carolina coast, two types of barnacles are commonly found (diagram 7): 1) Acorn Barnacles are the type seen on boat bottoms and tidal rocks. The name Acorn comes from a superficial resemblance to acorns of oak trees. 2) Goose Barnacles resemble Acorn Barnacles, except they occur on the end of a flexible stalk. Goose Barnacles are so-named because the ancient Greeks believed that geese arose spontaneously from these "goose-neck" barnacles.

Like mollusks (clam-like and snail-like animals), barnacles possess a

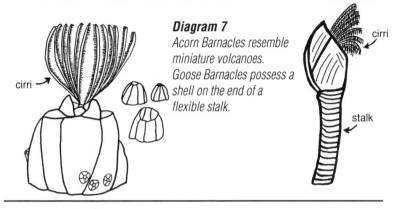

Diagram 7
Acorn Barnacles resemble miniature volcanoes. Goose Barnacles possess a shell on the end of a flexible stalk.

cirri

cirri

stalk

soft body surrounded by a hard shell. The resemblance is superficial, though, as barnacles are more closely related to fellow crustaceans such as shrimp and lobsters.

Like other crustaceans, barnacles molt in order to grow. Atypically, the outer shell is not cast off during molting. Instead, the covering of the inner soft parts are replaced. The outer shell continually enlarges to accommodate growth of the inner parts.

In some parts of the world, larger species of goose barnacles are eaten. For the most part, though, man regards barnacles as destructive nuisances. Barnacles hasten the rotting of pilings or other wooden objects in the water. More importantly, they attach to ship bottoms, increasing drag, decreasing speed, and increasing fuel consumption. Barnacles cost the U.S. shipping industry more than $100 million a year. Perhaps shippers should be glad for snails, as they prey on barnacles.

Interestingly, barnacles were one of the main interests of Charles Darwin, the originator of natural selection and evolution theory. Darwin spent eight years of his life studying and categorizing barnacles.

When a human is cut by a barnacle, the treatment of the wound is a medical challenge; these cuts heal slowly, and tend to become easily infected. Aggressive measures must be taken to avoid and treat infection, including thorough cleaning of the wound and use of antibiotics. The best medicine, though, is preventive — care should be taken crossing slippery tidal rocks or swimming near pilings.

MOLE CRAB

picture 33

Mole Crabs are small, egg-shaped, grayish-tan animals that inhabit the surf zone of sandy ocean beaches. Other names that Mole Crabs go by include Beach Fleas, Sand Crabs, Sand Fiddlers, and Sand Bugs. They are not "true" crabs but crustaceans, as are crabs, lobsters, and shrimp.

A Mole Crab can be safely picked up and examined in the palm of one's hand — they do not have pincers. Female crabs grow to one inch, twice the size of one-half inch males. Similar to true crabs, Mole Crabs have eyes located on the ends of movable stalks. The legs and posterior triangular telson of Mole Crabs are adapted for digging in sand. In the warm season, female Mole Crabs often carry a large mass of orange eggs on their underside.

Along with Coquina Clams, Mole Crabs are one of the dominant species found in the intertidal zone (between high and low tide water marks) on ocean beaches. Their presence in this area is sporadic, but, when found, they occur in great numbers.

Mole Crabs are continually moving with waves breaking on the beach. As a wave comes in, it shifts the sand where Mole Crabs are buried, exposing them. Very quickly, the crabs bury themselves again; by burying themselves, they avoid being swept out to sea and protect themselves from predators.

Immediately after burying itself, a Mole Crab sticks a pair of plumed antennae out of the sand (diagram 8); the antennae sift through the receding wave, filtering out particles of food and sand. Mouth parts of the Mole Crab remove particles trapped on the antennae, and both food and sand are swallowed. The task of separating and digesting the tiny plants and animals that live among the sand grains is left to the internal organs of the Mole Crab. This method of eating contrasts with animals such as Fiddler Crabs, which separate the particles of food from sand before eating.

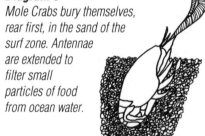

Diagram 8
Mole Crabs bury themselves, rear first, in the sand of the surf zone. Antennae are extended to filter small particles of food from ocean water.

Mole Crabs are thus constantly burrowing and migrating up and down the beach slope with rising and falling tides. Each wave is both friend and foe to the Mole Crab — bringing it food in the form of plankton, yet threatening to carry the Mole Crab out to sea or expose it to predators.

Burrowing is not the only protection Mole Crabs have against predators. Camouflage provided by their tan color allows Mole Crabs to blend effectively into the beach habitat.

Mole Crabs form an important link in many food chains. Numerous larger animals prey on Mole Crabs, including shorebirds, Blue Crabs, Ghost Crabs and fish. Sanderlings and Willets work the waves on the beach, searching for Mole Crabs. Mole Crabs, in turn, feed upon microscopic plankton.

The eggs of female Mole Crabs make the crabs especially inviting to fish. Surf fishermen use Mole Crabs to catch Kingfish (Whiting), Pompano, Red Drum, and Sheepshead. Fishermen often use a sieve-basket to scoop sand at the surf's edge; if Mole Crabs are present, one or two scoops may gather enough bait for a whole day.

In winter months, Mole Crabs disappear from the beach, heading for the bottom in deeper water. Mole Crabs have a relatively short lifespan: Males die shortly after mating, while many females die shortly after their eggs hatch.

Mole Crabs are edible. Hundreds (one to two pounds) must be gathered to make a meal. The Mole Crabs are steamed to make broth for an interesting chowder.

SHRIMP

picture 36

Shrimp, like lobsters, crayfish, and crabs, are crustaceans. That is, they have segmented bodies, jointed legs, stalked eyes, and hard external skeletons.

There are many types of shrimp and shrimp-like animals in Carolina waters. Three shrimp species, however, account for the catch of the commercial fishing industry and represent what most people think of as shrimp. These are the Brown, White, and Pink Shrimps (they come in colors, just like people).

The colors shrimp are named for are subtle hues, not vivid tones; these creatures are all translucent to some extent.

Female shrimp, which grow a little larger than males, can reach over eight inches in length. The large tail of a shrimp makes up about two-thirds of its length and weight; the tail, of course, is the part that is eaten by man.

Shrimp have 19 sets of paired appendages, including antennae for feeling, jaws for eating, jaw-feet for feeding, legs for walking, swimmerets and a tail fan for swimming.

The appendages of shrimp allow them to move by several methods. Shrimp can walk forward on the bottom, or they can swim forward slowly, using their swimmerets. In addition, when threatened, shrimp can swim rapidly backward by flipping their tail.

Shrimp thrive not only because of diverse methods of locomotion, but also because they consume a widely-varied diet (compare their success to seagulls' for the same reasons). Being both scavengers and omnivores, shrimp will eat almost anything. Their diet includes algae, decaying matter, worms, crabs, and small fish. Shrimp also eat their own molted shell, using it as a source of calcium to harden their new shell.

Molting is what allows a shrimp to grow larger. A shrimp's hard shell, or external skeleton, can't expand as the internal soft body of the shrimp grows; the shell must be replaced periodically with a larger shell. Interestingly, when a shrimp molts, it sheds not only its shell but also its stomach lining and terminal intestinal tract. The shrimp is most vulnerable to predators right after it molts, when its soft shell is still hardening.

Shrimp are found in depths from the low-tide line to 300 feet. In the fall, as temperatures drop, shrimp move to deeper water. With warm weather, they return to shallow water.

Adult shrimp migrate to the ocean to spawn. Newly-hatched shrimp are free-floating zooplankton. They eventually metamorphose into juvenile shrimp, which return to estuaries to feed and grow.

Older coastal residents recall years that shrimp were known as "bugs" and not widely consumed. Today, of course, shrimp are a highly popular menu item. In the last ten years, shrimp consumption in the United States has nearly doubled!

The increased shrimp eaten by Americans consists of imported, farmed shrimp. Shrimp ponds in tropical countries have proliferated; foreign aquaculturists generate several times the number of shrimp harvested by U.S. commercial fishing. The yield of shrimp by domestic net fishing has remained relatively constant over the past ten years.

SPINY LOBSTER
picture 37

Lobsters, like crabs, are crustaceans. Lobsters differ from crabs in having a large abdomen (tail) stretched out behind them (the smaller abdomen of crabs wraps under the crab's body).

The Spiny Lobster differs from the better-known Northern (Maine) Lobster in several respects. The smaller Spiny Lobster is a warm-water species, thriving in southern U.S. and Caribbean waters; the Northern Lobster rarely occurs south of Virginia. A Spiny Lobster has a spiny carapace and no claws; the Northern Lobster has a smooth carapace and a large pair of pincers (diagram 9).

Diagram 9
Spiny Lobster are protected by spines on their shell and antennae but lack claws. Northern Lobster possess large pincers.

Spiny Lobsters grow to two feet or more in length and weigh up to 30 pounds. They are tan-brown in color; pairs of light yellow or white spots highlight the tail.

Though clawless, the Spiny Lobster is protected by numerous strong spines on its shell and antennae. A prominent spine arches over each eye. The antennae are long, stretching the length of the lobster's body.

During the day, Spiny Lobsters hide in crevices on reefs and ledges. At night, they venture forth to feed on worms, mollusks, and carrion. Spiny Lobsters range from shallow water to depths of 300 feet.

Like crayfish, lobsters move either by walking slowly on their legs or swimming backwards rapidly by flipping their tail.

Every autumn, Spiny Lobsters exhibit an unusual migration. They walk along the ocean bottom in single file, maintaining contact with their antennae; groups of up to 60 lobsters head to deeper water for reasons unknown. The marching lobsters travel up to 30 miles over several days.

Lobsters produce planktonic larvae, shaped very differently from adults; after several months, the young animals undergo metamorphosis to adult form. Like other crustaceans, lobsters must molt to grow. Breeding size of eight to ten inches is attained at about five years of age. Full-grown size is reached in about 18 years.

Like Northern Lobsters, Spiny Lobsters have been overharvested. As a result, large lobsters are scarce; smaller specimens, up to 15 inches, are common.

The tail of a Spiny Lobster is the edible portion of the animal. Like crayfish or Northern Lobster, Spiny Lobster meat has a unique and excellent taste.

*The state seashell
of South Carolina
is the Olive Shell.*

 *The state seashell
of North Carolina
is the Scotch Bonnet.*

SHELLS

Seashells are made by mollusks. By definition, mollusks are invertebrate animals that produce shells of one or two pieces which wholly or partly enclose a soft body.

Shells are, in essence, the skeletons of mollusks. Like the internal skeleton (endoskeleton) of humans, the external skeleton (exoskeleton) of mollusks functions both for protection and as a site for muscle attachment.

A thin sac of tissue surrounds the internal organs of a mollusk. This sac, called the mantle, secretes the mollusk's shell. Calcium carbonate is absorbed from sea water, then secreted by glands in the mantle to produce and enlarge the shell. The colors of a shell are formed by pigment cells in the mantle.

A shell found on the beach, then, is the skeletal remnant of a dead mollusk. The shell remained with its soft-bodied creator until the mollusk died (mollusks do not grow new shells or change shells).

Shells with live animals inside are found less often. Live specimens are usually located in shallow waters of the ocean or sounds. Sometimes, the mollusk itself is inside the shell. More often, the shell is occupied by a hermit crab that inherited the shell from a dead mollusk.

A seashell exposed to the surf slowly erodes, adding particles to the beach and releasing minerals back into the ocean.

The shell-producing mollusks are divided into two main groups*: 1) Bivalves are clam-like animals with two shells, and 2) Gastropods (univalves) are snail-like animals with one shell.

The two shells of a **bivalve** are held tightly together when the animal is

---

Another group of mollusks, the cephalopods, includes squid and octopuses; these animals lack external shells, possessing internal or rudimentary shells.

alive; the shells are attached along the hinge by a ligament, and strong adductor muscles pull the shell closed. Round or oval muscle scars, where adductor muscles attach, are often visible on the inside of washed-up shells (diagram 10).

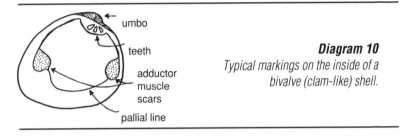

Diagram 10
Typical markings on the inside of a bivalve (clam-like) shell.

The two parts of a bivalve shell are most often mirror images of each other. The animal inside is often an indistinct blob; unlike a gastropod, a bivalve possesses neither head nor radula; the foot may be well-developed or not.

A snail-like **gastropod**, on the other hand, normally has a large muscular foot and a well-developed head with distinct eyes, mouth, and tentacles (diagram 11). The foot and head of a gastropod are extended and withdrawn through the aperture (opening) of its one-piece shell. Most often, the gastropod has a round, thin piece of shell called an operculum attached to its foot; the operculum is used to close the aperture when the animal retreats inside its shell.

Diagram 11
A snail-like gastropod has a distinct foot, head, mouth, eyes, and tentacles.

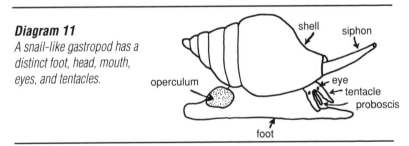

A gastropod also has a radula, a tongue-like, toothed appendage (diagram 12). The radula is adapted to bore, saw, tear, or scrape, depending on the feeding habits of the species.

Bivalve and gastropod species are prolific and widespread. Over 100,000 living species exist worldwide. More than 1,000 types of shell-bearing mollusks live in coastal Carolina waters. Only the species whose shells commonly appear on Carolina beaches are included in the following sections.

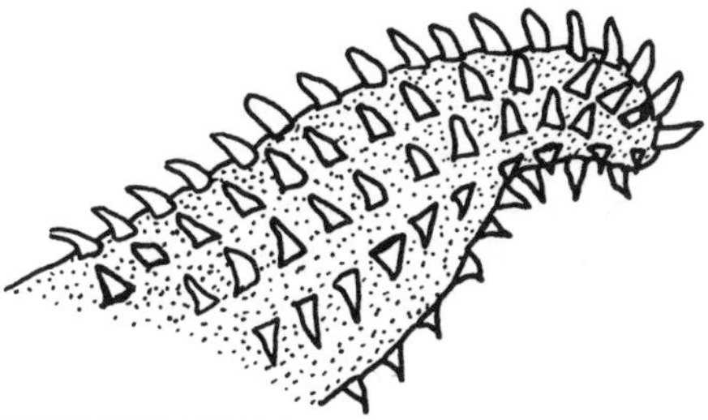

Diagram 12
The tongue-like radula of gastropods is used to bore, saw, or scrape while feeding.

Finding attractive shells on the beach is often a matter of persistence and luck. In general, though, beachcombing is better at low tide, after a storm, and on isolated beaches.

ANGEL WING

picture 38

Most seashells are sturdy and survive the pounding surf a bit worn but intact. Angel Wings, on the other hand, are fragile shells that often chip or crack before reaching the beach. If an intact specimen (one shell of the bivalve) is found, it must be packed with care to survive a trip home.

Angel Wing shells are chalky white in color and measure four to eight inches in length. On the exterior, about 30 spiny, radial ribs are crossed by much fainter concentric growth lines. On the inside, a spoon-shaped appendage projects from the hinge area; the spoon is where the animal's foot muscles attach to the shell.

Living Angel Wings are bivalves; both sides of the shell are identical. When the two sides of the white shell open, they resemble a pair of angel wings.

The foot of an Angel Wing mollusk is well-developed, enabling the animal to burrow into sand or mud. Angel Wings live buried in the ocean or sound bottom; they obtain food by siphoning water down into their shell. Angel Wings are found from the low tide mark to around 60 feet deep.

Several other species of Angel Wings are found in the Carolinas, smaller in size but similar in shape. Like many other bivalves, Angel Wings are edible.

ARK SHELL

picture 39

Ark shells are among the most abundant shells found on Carolina beaches. The shape of ark shells is what best distinguishes them; perhaps the best description of their shape is "an off-center clam." One side of the clam-like shell is definitely larger.

Ark shells are further characterized by linear ribs on the outside, running from the hinge area to the periphery. Ark species range in size from one-half to four inches.

Inside ark shells, the straight hinge line is marked by small teeth. Two round areas where adductor muscles attach are often visible.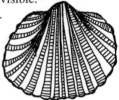
Adductor muscles function to close the shell tightly. Ark shells also show the scar of the mantle outlined inside the shell; the mantle scar is a slightly raised white area, with distinct borders, extending almost to the periphery of the shell. The mantle is the fleshy sac that surrounds the internal organs of the clam-like animal living in the shell, and it secretes the animal's shell.

Live ark shells are covered with a dark, hairy layer called the periostracum. The periostracum is sometimes partially intact when ark shells wash up on the beach.

Ark shells live on the ocean or sound bottom in locations ranging from tidal flats to offshore depths. More than ten species of ark shells are found in Carolina waters. Identification is aided by teeth and rib counts.

AUGER SHELL
picture 40

An auger shell is small, long and narrow. The shell consists of numerous whorls which taper to a point at one end. There is a large opening on the big end of the shell.

The Common Auger, also known as the Atlantic Auger, is the species most often found on Carolina beaches. It reaches two inches in length, and the color varies from light tan to gray or even orange. There are 12 to 15 whorls on the shell. The snail-like animal residing in the shell eats worms, engulfing them with its proboscis (a tube-like part of the mouth).

The Concave Auger is one of several other species found in the Carolinas. Like most augers, the Concave Auger has a poison gland on its tongue-like radula, which it uses to paralyze the worms it preys upon.

CLAM (QUAHOG)
picture 41

The shell of the Quahog (pronounced co-hog) Clam is commonly found on Carolina beaches; the species is also known as the Hard-shelled Clam.

The Quahog shell is easily recognized; the outside is tan to whitish, with fine concentric rings. The shell feels thick, heavy, and solid. Sometimes, two clam shells are found still attached at the hinge (the live clam is a bivalve, having two symmetrical shells).

On closer inspection, the shell is broadly oval in shape, with a thicker, prominent umbo (hinged end). The concentric rings become more prominent toward the outer edge of the shell.

The inside of a Quahog shell has several distinct markings. A variable amount of purple color is often present on part of the outer edge. Two oval scars of the adductor muscles (which hold the clam shut) can be seen on either side. The dull, chalky white center is surrounded by a smooth and shiny surface; the outer edge has fine serrations.

The Quahog Clam's body has a soft, irregular shape. With its strong foot, the clam burrows into mud and sand on bay and inlet bottoms where it lives. The clam protects itself by closing its shell tightly with two strong adductor muscles. To feed, the clam opens its shell and extends a siphon apparatus up to the water.

The siphon apparatus allows the clam to filter-feed; the filter system consists of two tubes, an incurrent siphon and an excurrent siphon, along with gills. Water is drawn in through the incurrent siphon; it then passes over the clam's gills, where oxygen and plankton are removed. Water is then ejected through the excurrent siphon, along with rejected debris and wastes.

This filtering mechanism, used to feed on plentiful microorganisms in water, has enabled clams and oysters to successfully inhabit the earth for millions and millions of years. However, the filtering mechanism also makes them susceptible to man's recent proliferation and intrusion into coastal areas. Increased silt in the water, caused by dredging, can suffocate clams if sand and mud particles cannot be eliminated fast enough. And more bacteria, inevitable with increasing human population, result in the contamination of shellfish — clams and oysters also filter and concentrate harmful bacteria.

The concentration of bacteria by clams' superior filter-feeding mechanism can also affect humans. In an ironic cycle, man can acquire diseases from eating clams and oysters contaminated as a result of human development.

While Quahogs consume microorganisms, they are preyed upon by larger animals, such as moon snails, oyster drills, whelks, and sea stars (starfish). Moon snails and oyster drills bore through the thick clam shells with their tongue-like radulas, while whelks and sea stars forcefully pry open the clam's shells.

If Quahogs manage to survive predators (including the supreme predator, man), they can live up to 40 years, growing to over six inches long.

Clams reproduce by shedding sperm and eggs directly into open water, so fertilization is haphazard. Prodigious numbers of gametes are released to ensure success, however; one female may release up to 24 million eggs during a single spawning!

Native American Indians found many uses for Quahogs. The Algonquin Indians, who gave the Quahog its name, used the meat for food and the shells for tools and ornaments. In addition, Indians made beads from

Quahog shells, which were strung together as wampum (shell money). Wampum beads from the purple portion of the Quahog shell were valued two to four times higher than wampum from the white portion.

Quahog Clams are prized yet today, as evidenced by a large commercial fishery. Typically, Quahogs are raked by hand or taken with mechanical harvesters on boats.

Quahogs sold commercially are labeled by size, though the terminology is not consistent from state to state. Generally, Littlenecks and Cherrystones are smaller clams, about one and a half and two inches, respectively. Chowder clams are bigger Quahogs, three inches or larger. The smaller varieties are more tender and can be eaten whole — raw, steamed, or cooked in any recipe. The larger clams are less tender and are usually chopped before using in chowder or other dishes.

COCKLE SHELL
picture 42

Cockle shells are among the larger and sturdier shells found on Carolina beaches; bigger specimens measure five inches in diameter.

Cockles are "classic seashell" oval in shape. On the outside of the shell, there are prominent radial ribs, running from the hinge area to the edges. Cockles are equivalves, meaning both shells of the bivalve are equal.

Upon close inspection, the inside of the shell has radial grooves. Two faint oval muscle scars (where the adductor muscles that close the shell attach) are seen. Near the hinge area, there is one central tooth and one or two lateral teeth. The edges of the shell are scalloped.

Cockle shells have proliferated on earth for at least 65 million years (man has been here the last one-half percent of this time). While more than 200 species exist worldwide, only about seven are found on Carolina beaches.

Plankton and detritus (small particles of decaying matter) make up the cockle's diet. After burrowing into the ocean or sound bottom, the cockle extends siphons above the sand and draws in sea water. An internal mucus device adsorbs plankton, which is passed to the mouth.

The most common cockle shell in the Carolinas is the Giant Atlantic Cockle; it grows up to five inches in length. This species is also known as the Great Heart Cockle (two shells held together form the shape of a heart). The outside of the shell is dirty-white to tan, with darker red-brown spots, often in rings. Upon close inspection, the outside ribs have scale-like ridges.

The Giant Atlantic Cockle ranges from the shallows of the surf to 100 feet deep. Like other cockles, it has a strong muscular foot used for rapid burrowing in the sand or moving across sandy bottoms.

The Prickly Cockle is also commonplace on Carolina beaches and tidal flats. Smaller than the Giant Atlantic Cockle, it grows to two and one-half inches in size. This species is distinguished by small prickly spines on its ribs.

The Yellow Cockle and Atlantic Strawberry Cockle are also found in large numbers on some Carolina beaches.

It is interesting that cockles are frequently eaten in European countries, raw or cooked. In the U.S., they are not widely used, though some Americans make an excellent cockle chowder.

COQUINA CLAM
picture 43

Coquina Clam shells are among the smallest shells found on the beach. At the same time, they are certainly among the most attractive. Coquinas are usually one-half to three-fourths inch long; they are wedge-shaped, sort of a triangle with rounded edges. Coquinas are bivalves, with two identical shells.

Coquina shells are spectacular because they come in a variable rainbow spectrum of colors and patterns (thus the scientific name *variabilis*). The outside of the shell may be white, blue, yellow, brown, red, etc., in a solid, rayed, or ringed pattern.

The combination of colors and patterns is truly limitless. The colors inside the shell also vary tremendously and they may or may not match the outside color of the shell.

The intertidal zone, the area of beach between high and low tide, is the sole place Coquina Clams live. They exist in dense groups, with up to 1,500 clams in a single square foot of beach.

A beachcomber often notices Coquinas burying themselves in the sand as a wave recedes. When a wave washes in, it shifts the sand, exposing the tiny clams. To protect themselves, Coquinas quickly dig back into the sand.

Like most clams, Coquinas strain seawater, feeding on plankton. They lie buried in the sand, less than one inch from the surface; the ends of two siphons extend slightly above the surface of the sand (diagram 13). The siphons circulate seawater, and plankton is removed with a mucus device.

Diagram 13
Coquinas live buried in sand of the surf zone. The tiny clams extend siphons above the sand, feeding on plankton filtered from ocean water.

At times, Coquinas appear to be popping up in the sand — they are actually reburying themselves. When a Coquina is exposed by waves, its white foot juts from its shell; the foot pulls the shell upright, and the animal rapidly burrows back into the sand. This rapid reburial can be observed close hand if a Coquina and a small amount of sand are placed in the palm of one's hand.

Looking closely at a Coquina shell, the inside edge is grooved. The outside of the shell reveals tiny radial ribs on the shorter end, which gradually fade in the longer end. The ribs fade because the longer (foot) end of the shell is constantly being dug into the sand, wearing away the grooves.

Coquinas are edible; numerous Coquinas are boiled to make broth for a fine chowder. Also, Coquina stone, made of compacted dead shells, is used in parts of the world as building material. Coquina stone is found on some Carolina beaches.

Other names for Coquinas include Wedge Clams (wedge-shaped) and Butterflies (the two shells of a Coquina look like butterfly wings when spread apart).

CROSS-BARRED VENUS CLAM

picture 44

Shells of the Cross-barred Venus Clam are plentiful on Carolina beaches. They are small, ranging from one-half to two inches. The color is typically white, with an occasional shell exhibiting faint brown radial stripes.

The gridwork pattern on the outside of the Venus Clam shell is distinctive and attractive; radial ribs are crossed by concentric ridges to produce the cross-barred design.

Inside the shell, there is a central white area where the mantle of the clam attaches. On either side of the mantle remnant, there are two roundish areas where adductor muscles attach. Two prominent projections or "teeth" are present on the hinge, and the outer lip has very fine ridges.

The Cross-barred Clam lives in the sand of eelgrass beds. Densities as high as 150 clams per square meter have been documented. The clam feeds by filtering plankton from seawater, using a siphon system to move water over a mucus collecting net.

Another name for this species is the Dog Clam. Like its clam-family relatives, the Cross-barred Clam is edible, and makes an excellent chowder.

DISK SHELL
picture 45

Disk Shells are members of the clam family. They are white, flattened, and nearly circular. Disk Shells range up to three inches in size. One other feature makes Disk Shells stand out on the seashore: Their hinge ligament is so tough that they often wash up on the beach with both sides of the shell still connected.

Looking closely at the outside of the shell, there are numerous fine concentric ridges, similar to the ridges on a record album. A translucent, varnish-like layer (periostracum) covers the shell; this thin layer may be partially worn away, revealing the brighter white shell underneath.

The inside of a Disk Shell shows the faint, chalky white outline of the mantle. At the hinge, two or three grooves and teeth (raised ridges) are seen; the grooves and hinges interlock with matching structures on the other half of the shell.

Disk Shells live in sounds, shallow-water sandflats, and offshore sandy areas. They burrow into the sand and extend their siphons upward to feed.

JINGLE SHELL
picture 46

Thin, translucent, variously-colored Jingle Shells are distinctive and common on the beaches of North and South Carolina. These shells are irregularly round or oval in shape, three-fourths to two inches in diameter. Colors include white, tan, gold, silver, and black; shells that are buried in mud and sand take on darker colors. Variability in color, translucency (see-through appearance), and shininess make Jingles interesting and attractive.

The Jingle Shell is a bivalve, but the two sides of the shell are not identical.

The top shell is the half of the Jingle Shell that is commonly found on the beach; it is convex in shape. The exterior has faint circular growth lines. The interior of the shell is shiny, except for a central dull-white area; this irregular chalky area often has the shape of a baby's foot. Three round muscle scars are often visible inside the white portion.

The bottom shell is smaller, flat, and has a hole near the hinge. Through this hole passes the byssus, a calcareous plug that attaches the animal to hard objects such as oyster shells, rocks, wood, and coral. The bottom shell is found on the beach much less frequently, as it often remains attached to the bottom, and is more fragile than the top shell.

Only the top shell moves as the clam-like animal opens and closes its shell to gather food on its cilia; the bottom shell is fixed firmly in position.

Sailors of olden days called Jingle Shells "Mermaid's Toenails." Jingles are eaten in Europe. In the U.S., the shells are made into wind chimes.

The Jingle poem expresses beachcombers' delight in Jingle Shells particularly well:

We collect the Jingle Shell so numerous
By means of ulna, radius, and humerus,
And bring them to creative dreamers
On tired tibias and fibulas and femurs.

KEYHOLE LIMPET
picture 47

A Keyhole Limpet shell resembles a tiny, Chinese coolie's hat, or a miniature volcano. It is small, oval in shape, and has a single hole at its peak.

The name of the Keyhole Limpet stems from the shape of the hole: It often resembles a keyhole. The hole functions to drain water after it has passed over the gills of the Limpet.

Looking closely at a Limpet shell, distinct radial ribs run from the hole to the bottom rim. The color is off-white but may be obscured by a green algal slime on fresh specimens.

The Limpet is a gastropod, or snail-like animal (diagram 14). Thus, it is a univalve (one shell), unlike a clam with two shells (bivalve). The keyhole opening is not at the top of the shell in baby Limpets; the opening begins as a slit near the edge of the shell and migrates to the top as the animal grows.

Keyhole Limpets live on solid objects such as rocks, pilings, and jetties. The Limpet uses its tongue-like radula to hollow out a small depression in the rock or wood. The Limpet spends most of the daytime settled firmly in this hollowed-out space. At night, the Limpet crawls about on its large suction-like foot. The Limpet moves only short distances, grazing on a vegetarian diet of algae.

The Keyhole Limpet is well-adapted to its environment. If a falling tide leaves the Limpet out of water, it shuts tight; the Limpet can survive high and dry for hours. A Limpet also endures the force of waves pounding the rocks and pilings it lives on. The conical shape helps a Limpet cling to its base; the waves actually push the Limpet down harder on its substrate instead of washing it away.

Sexes are separate among Keyhole Limpets. Eggs are laid on the rocks where Limpets live. Adults may reach up to two inches in size.

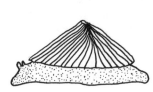 

Diagram 14
A limpet is a gastropod (snail-like animal). The shell resembles a miniature volcano.

KITTEN'S PAW
picture 47

The Kitten's Paw is well-named; the shell does indeed resemble the foot of a kitten. It is fan-shaped, up to one and a half inches long, with five to seven distinct wavy ribs on the outside. The color is white, with red-brown markings between or on the ridges. The shell is thick, like that of its close relative, the oyster. The interior of the shell is white, save for one dark oval where the single adductor muscle attaches to the shell.

A mollusk lives inside and produces the two shells of a Kitten's Paw (it is a bivalve). Living specimens are cemented to rocks or shells, from the low tide line to 300 feet deep.

MARSH PERIWINKLE
picture 48

Marsh Periwinkles, also known as Marsh Snails, are acorn-sized snails seen crawling on marsh grass.

On close inspection, a Marsh Periwinkle shell is one inch or less in diameter. It is spiral in shape, with circular grooves covering the shell. The color is gray-white, but the shell is often partly obscured by green algal slime. There is an orange streak on one side of the shell opening.

The snail-like animal (gastropod) living in the shell has two tentacles on its head, with an eye at the base of each; the proboscis, or nose, is between the tentacles. The male exhibits a prominent penis behind the right tentacle in the breeding season.

The only habitat of the Marsh Periwinkle is salt marsh, as the snail is dependent upon brackish water.

The Marsh Periwinkle is a herbivore, feeding on algae that grows on marsh grass, rocks, shells, debris, and the marsh surface itself. The snail uses its radula, a tongue-like structure, to feed. The radula has up to 300 rows of teeth and is pulled back and forth across a surface, like a rasp on wood. The constant grinding wears away the radula teeth at the rate of five to six rows a day; the teeth are continually replaced, much like sharks' teeth.

Few animals compete with Marsh Snails, so they often populate salt marshes in great numbers. In winter, the thin leaves of marsh grass are conspicuously absent of Periwinkles; the snails abound in the marsh only in warmer weather.

Many shorebirds feed on Marsh Periwinkles. They are also eaten by man. If one takes time to cook Periwinkles, the reward will be small tidbits of escargot (from the French, meaning "an edible snail"). Periwinkles are prepared by cleaning them in fresh water, then steaming for about 10 minutes. The meat inside the shell is picked out with a small toothpick and dipped in butter.

Marsh Periwinkles should not be confused with inedible Mud Snails. Mud Snails are small black snails found in great numbers on mud flats, often under water.

MOON SHELL (SHARK EYE)
picture 49

The Moon Shell is a gastropod, a snail-like animal with a single spiral shell. Moon Shells are aptly named, with their smooth, gray to tan, spherical shells; they range from one-quarter to five inches in diameter. The most common member of this family, the Atlantic Moon Snail, is also known as the Shark Eye. The darker central whorl and eyeball shape give it the appearance of an eye.

The person that picked the name Shark Eye was probably unaware that the Moon Snail family has more in common with sharks than appearance. Moon Snails are, in fact, voracious predators, just like sharks. They attack other mollusks, especially clams. Moon Snails drill a hole through the shell of their prey using a radula, a tongue-like apparatus with teeth on it. A Moon Snail pulls its rasp-like radula back and forth, secreting an acidic substance that softens the shell at the same time. Once the hole penetrates the shell, the Moon Snail is able to suck out the flesh of the mollusk. Using this method, a Moon Snail can eat as many as four clams a day!

In order to find mollusks to prey upon, a Moon Snail must actively move about. To do so, it extends a broad snail-like foot through the sand; the rest of the body and shell is then pulled forward. This form of locomotion leaves distinctive trails on the ocean or sound bottom.

While the Moon Snail feeds on valuable clams and oysters (and even its own kind), it has its own place in the food chain. Sea stars (starfish), oyster drills, and bottom-feeding fish are among its predators.

Shells are not all that Moon Snails leave on ocean beaches; their "sand collar" egg cases are also found by beachcombers. The female Moon Snail lays her eggs in a mass formed out of a gelatinous material and sand. When this mass (diagram 15) washes up on the beach, it is said to resemble a detachable shirt collar (as used in Victorian times or by clergymen today). Another more common object the egg case resembles is the rubber end of a "plumber's helper," used to unclog toilets and drains.

Diagram 15
Moon Snail egg cases sometimes wash up on beaches.

MUD SNAIL
picture 50

Mud Snails are found in great numbers on tidal mud flats. The sheer abundance of these animals is what makes them noticeable, as their individual appearance is rather unspectacular.

A Mud Snail's shell is small, less than an inch in length; the color is dull black. The top of the Mud Snail shell ends in a spire; often, the spire is worn down at the tip. Usually, the shell is covered with a slimy green-brown growth, which obscures the shell surface and makes the shell slippery to touch. Both the underlying color and the covering growth effectively camouflage the Mud Snail in its environment.

The color of the snail's body is off-white. Patches of green-brown growth highlight and camouflage the snail's body; the bottom of the snail's foot is free of growth. The shell opening often has a dark purplish hue. If a live snail is not inside the shell, then a small hermit crab has likely established residence.

Mud Snail is an appropriate name, as the animals live on the muddy bottom of tidal flats. The snails congregate in small tidal pools when the tide is out; at times, they burrow into the muddy substrate. In this manner, they avoid drying out at low tide.

Mud Snails are hardy: The twice-daily ebb and flow of tides on mud flats means the snails must withstand wide variations in water level, temperature and salinity.

As they crawl along the bottom, Mud Snails leave small grooves in the mud. They feed as they travel, consuming mud and microscopic plant life. Given the opportunity, though, Mud Snails readily eat decaying animal flesh. In fact, they are able to detect carrion (decaying flesh) at long distances; Mud Snails possess a very sensitive chemoreceptor sense of smell. Swarms of Mud Snails gather quickly to consume a dead crab or fish in a tidal flat.

In turn, Mud Snails are preyed upon by fish such as Puffers and Oyster Toads; numerous species of waterfowl and wading birds also feast on Mud Snails.

Several species of flatworms parasitize Mud Snails. One worm, a blood fluke, parasitizes shorebirds in its adult stage; this species does not parasitize humans to cause serious harm, but exposure can result in "swimmer's itch" or "clammer's itch." The larvae of the flatworms penetrate the skin of people wading in the marsh; the worm can burrow in layers of skin for several days before dying. If a person is sensitive to the worms, a pattern of small red lines appears in the skin; the area can be intensely pruritic (itchy). Symptomatic treatment is adequate: Hydrocortisone cream rubbed onto the area and diphenhydramine (benadryl) by mouth suffice.

Mud Snails are similar to Marsh Periwinkles in several respects: Both are small, nondescript gastropods (snails) found in large numbers in their respective habitats. Mud Snails should not be confused with Marsh Periwinkles, though, for unlike Periwinkles, Mud Snails are not edible.

MUSSEL
picture 51

Mussels are bivalve mollusks; the two shells of a mussel are equal in size and typically fan-shaped.

Mussels are noted for their byssal threads, clusters of strong fibers that attach them to rocks or plants (diagram 16).

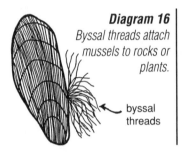

Diagram 16
Byssal threads attach mussels to rocks or plants.

byssal threads

The Ribbed Mussel is the most common species in the Carolinas. Up to five inches in length, its shell is wide and rounded on one end, narrow and pointed at the other end. Prominent radial ribs on the outside of the shell give it its name. The exterior is white but usually obscured by an olive-brown layer, the periostracum. The inside of the shell has a definite "footstep" shape. The smooth, shiny lining of a Ribbed Mussel shell is a beautiful silver-white, tinged with purple and blue — quite a contrast to the dull, ribbed exterior. The hinge of the Ribbed Mussel is located on its narrow end. A single adductor muscle closes the upper end of the shell.

The Ribbed Mussel lives in salt marshes and brackish estuaries. Its byssal threads anchor it among roots of spartina marshgrass; the Mussel lies buried except for an inch of its wide end, which sticks above the mud. The mollusk opens its shell at high tide and feeds by siphoning water; at low tide the shell is closed tight. Somehow, the Ribbed Mussel survives even in polluted waters.

Ribbed Mussels are edible; when steamed, Ribbed Mussels are chewier and fuller-flavored than oysters. The presence of large numbers of Ribbed Mussel shells in Indian digs indicates they were a staple in coastal Indians' diet.

The Blue Mussel is prized for its taste. Although this species is widespread, specimens are small south of Cape Hatteras. Blue Mussels are especially valued for food in Europe. Unlike the Ribbed Mussel, pollutants tend to concentrate in the Blue Mussel's body, affecting the mollusk and those eating it.

Mussels are able to move from place to place, albeit very slowly. Each time mussels change location, they must re-anchor themselves with new byssal threads.

Mussels secrete a glue which helps hold them to rocks, plants, or soft bottoms; the glue is very strong and, obviously, waterproof. The key ingredient of mussel glue has recently been synthesized, and it may have a future use in medicine, mending broken bones and other body parts.

OLIVE SHELL

picture 52

Olive Shells (South Carolina's state seashell) are cylindrical in shape; they reach up to three inches in length. The outside of the shell is smooth and shiny; the color is tan-gray, highlighted by brown zigzag markings. The zigzag designs are said to resemble script writing, and thus the nickname "Lettered Olive Shell." A short, pointed spire sticks out from one end. The opening of the shell is long and narrow, wider at the blunt end.

If a shell is found freshly washed up on the beach, the above description applies. If the shell lies on the beach, sun and surf wear it down quickly; the basic shape remains, but the gloss and markings fade, leaving a dull white finish.

The animal residing in the shell is a gastropod, a snail-like creature. Live Olive Shells inhabit sandy-bottom areas, from the low tide mark to 150 feet deep. They are carnivores, preying on bivalves such as clams, cockles, mussels, and Coquinas. The snails also scavenge, consuming carrion (dead animal flesh).

OYSTER

picture 53

Oyster shells are very common on ocean beaches. They vary in shape and color, unlike most other shells. In general, Oyster shells are long and narrow, ranging up to ten inches in length; the shells are thick and sturdy, with irregular ridges on the outside.

Inside, Oyster shells are smooth and often tinged with purple. The muscle scar, where the adductor muscle attaches, is typically dark purple. Single shells are found on the beach, but the living Oyster is a bivalve (mollusk with two shells).

Oysters thrive in water of low to medium salinity, as found in sounds and estuaries. They live in water depths from the low tide line to 40 feet. Oysters are sessile, meaning they do not move about their environment. In fact, oysters permanently cement themselves to hard objects.

Oysters are often located in clusters where they attach to each other; large numbers of clusters gathered in the same area make up an Oyster bed (also known as a rake).

The animal inside the shells is a fleshy, tan-gray blob. Unlike a clam, an Oyster has no developed foot for movement, no siphons, and one adductor muscle instead of two.

Interestingly, Oysters change sex repeatedly during their lives. Larger Oysters generally remain functional females. An average-sized female can release 100 million eggs at a time and spawn two to three times a season. Less than ten of the eggs probably reach maturity.

Fertilized eggs hatch into tiny animals that become free-floating zooplankton. Later, the spat (larval Oysters ready to attach) must find a hard surface to settle on to survive. If the spat find a shell or rock, they cement themselves to it. The spat exhibit a preference to attach to existing beds of oyster shells.

In three to five years, Oysters can reach three to four inches in length; eventually they can grow to 10 or even 12 inches long. Scientists estimate Oysters live 20 years or longer.

To feed, Oysters open their shells and fan water over internal gills; about seven gallons of water a day are filtered, and plankton and other microorganisms are extracted from the water. To some extent, Oysters are able to eject sand and mud particles taken in with their food. However, if they are overwhelmed, or covered with silt, they smother to death. Oysters are thus devastated by nearby dredging.

Because of their filter-feeding system, Oysters concentrate bacteria, and can be adversely affected by harmful bacteria. Oysters may die themselves or pass diseases to humans when eaten. Type A Hepatitis and bacterial gastroenteritis (intestinal infection) are among the diseases acquired by eating tainted shellfish.

Humans sometimes suffer from Oyster contact in another manner. The edges of Oyster shells are thin and razor sharp; when a barefoot wader steps on an Oyster shell, a deep, jagged cut results. The cut is often contaminated with sand, silt, and shell particles, so it is prone to infection. Lacerations from Oyster shells should be thoroughly cleaned, inside and out, to minimize chances of infection.

Animals preying on adult Oysters include sea stars (starfish), Oyster Drills, Moon Snails, rays, Oystercatchers, and man. The plankton and spat stages of Oysters, of course, are vulnerable to many animals.

Some enemies of adult Oysters, such as sea stars and Oyster Drills, are unable to tolerate areas of low salinity. Oysters, which tolerate a wide range of salinity, can escape these enemies by settling in areas of lower salt content (such as estuaries with less than 15 parts per thousand salt).

Man has harvested Oysters for thousands of years; piles of Oyster shells are common in ancient Indian ruins. Oysters remain commercially valuable today. Wild populations are gathered, and cultivated Oysters are farmed in artificial beds.

If a person is able to overcome the initial hesitation of eating a shapeless, slimy blob, Oysters are an unsurpassed delicacy. They are excellent raw, steamed, roasted, fried, or stewed.

The concept that Oysters are only in season during colder months (months with an R in them) is somewhat outdated. Refrigeration and Oyster farming make Oysters available year round now.

Some people cherish the taste of Oysters so much that they use certain phrases in front of others to lessen competition for them. Novice Oyster eaters tend to be discouraged by crude nicknames such as sliders, slime-doggies, snotters, and blob-boogers. In this manner, experienced Oyster consumers keep all the more Oysters to enjoy for themselves.

OYSTER DRILL
picture 54

Oyster Drill shells are fairly small, measuring less than two inches in length. They are spindle-shaped, with nine to twelve distinct ridges running from the top to the bottom of the shell. The ridges are crossed by finer lines circling the shell. Oyster Drills are typically tan or gray on the outside; inside the shell opening there is often purple coloration.

Living up to its name, the Oyster Drill is a significant predator on young oysters. The snail-like Oyster Drill literally drills into an oyster's shell and feeds on the oyster's soft body parts. This method of feeding may be labeled "eating oysters on the whole shell." Predation on oysters by Oyster Drills is a bigger problem in northern states than in the Carolinas.

Oyster Drills live on oyster beds, jetties, and pilings, located from the high tide line to about 50 feet deep. In such locations, they prey on barnacles and snails in addition to bivalves.

Oyster Drills are not able to tolerate salinities below 15 parts per thousand, and thus cannot prey on oysters in less salty water. Commercial oyster farmers often locate their oyster beds in areas of low salinity to avoid losing their "crop" to Oyster Drills.

PEN SHELL
picture 55

Pen Shells are among the largest shells washing up on Carolina beaches; they measure up to ten inches in length. The fan-shaped shells are rather thin and brittle. When they wash onto ocean beaches during winter storms, the fragile shells are often broken. If one is lucky, though, the Pen Shell is found intact. If one is very lucky, both shells of this bivalve may be found intact and still connected.

A Pen Shell burrows into a sandy or muddy bottom. The top of the shell remains exposed above the sand; the shell opens to feed on particles in the water. The bottom (narrow end) of the shell is anchored by byssal threads, which are very tough and durable.

Upon closer inspection, the inside of a Pen Shell is smooth and shiny. The outside of the shell has a shiny layer, often covered by a rougher, ridged layer. Frequently, barnacles, oysters, slipper shells, or other animals are attached to the outside of Pen Shells.

A Pen Shell is thin enough that if it is held up to the sun, one's hand can be seen through the shell. The brittleness of the shell is due not only to the thinness, but also to the very large size of the shell's prismatic crystals, which can be seen using a hand lens.

The thinness of the Pen Shell means that the shell is closed in a manner atypical of mollusks: When the shell's adductor muscles contract, the shell bends, bringing the edges together. When the muscles relax, the shell springs open again.

The meat of the Pen Shell is edible. The Pen Shell is also the only shellfish in our marine waters that produces a valuable pearl. In Mediterranean countries, the Pen Shell's tough byssal threads have been woven into cloth.

Pen shells of different species also live in estuary and sound waters of the Carolinas.

Tiny Oyster Crabs (Pea Crabs) often live in the mantle cavity of Pen Shells. The crabs are protected from predators and feed upon surplus food particles brought in by the Pen Shell. Small shrimp may likewise spend parts of their lives in the mantle cavities of Pen Shells. This type of arrangement, where one animal lives with another, benefiting from but not parasitizing its host, is called commensal habitation.

RAZOR CLAM
picture 55

Razor clams are long and narrow bivalves. They have a strong muscular foot that is used to burrow rapidly into sandy bottoms.

The Atlantic Jackknife Clam, or Atlantic Razor Clam, is the most easily recognized member of this group. It is aptly named, looking much like an old-fashioned straight razor. Measuring up to six inches in length, the Atlantic Jackknife is six times as long as it is wide. While living, the shell is covered with a shiny, greenish-brown layer, the periostracum; after the clam dies, the periostracum wears away, revealing the lighter white appearance of the underlying shell. Delicate growth rings are also visible on the shell.

Several smaller razor clams are found in the Carolinas as well. These species, known as Tagelus Razor Clams, are shorter, usually less than three inches in length; they are wider and more oval in shape.

Razor clams are named not only for their shape, but also for their sharpness: The edges of these shells can be "razor sharp," and Indians are reported to have shaved with them.

Razor clams are known for their ability to rapidly burrow into sand or mud. The clam-like animal digs by extending its foot deep into the sand, then pulling its shell down after it.

The burrow holes of razor clams can be found on intertidal beaches. The holes are small and oval, and have no sand or droppings piled outside (unlike crab holes).

As they are quite edible fried or cooked in a chowder, razor clams are collected by seafood connoisseurs. Razor clams can be gathered by digging them out of their burrows; one must be quick and quiet, however, as they are sensitive to vibrations and will burrow deeper to escape if they sense an intruder. One source reports that a razor clam can also be taken by putting a handful of salt into a burrow hole. The high salinity irritates the clam, causing it to rise up out of its hole; the clam must be grabbed quickly before it can retreat into its burrow.

SCALLOP

picture 56

Scallop shells are very common on Carolina beaches. A distinct form makes scallops easily identified; varied colors make them especially attractive.

Scallop shells have an oval shape typical of many seashells. They are distinguished, however, by the presence of extensions or "ears" on the hinge area (where the shells attach to each other). Scallop shells also have definite raised ridges, extending from the hinge to the edge of the shell.

The soft-bodied mollusk living inside the shells is similar to a clam. When viewed underwater, the shell opens slightly, and eyes and small tentacles are seen. The eyes are a ring of numerous bright blue dots around the edge of each shell. The tentacles are short extensions from the body, also at the edge of the shells.

Like clams, scallops feed on plankton filtered from seawater; but, unlike clams, scallops do not burrow beneath the bottom. Instead, they live in small hollows scooped out on the bottom.

Although scallops live not buried, but in the open, they are not defenseless: Scallops are able to move in their environment. Scallops swim by jet propulsion; they close their shell rapidly, expel a jet of water, and move off in the opposite direction. Adult scallops swim in this manner infrequently; they do so only when disturbed or to escape approaching predators such as sea stars (starfish).

The Atlantic Bay Scallop grows to three and one-half inches in length. Living in sounds or estuaries, it is fished commercially. The first stage of the Bay Scallop, like other scallops, exists as free-swimming zooplankton. The next stage of the Bay Scallop is sedentary, allowing the shell to grow. Usually, the scallop attaches by byssal threads to eelgrass in shallow water;

the scallop thus escapes being covered with silt on the bottom (and suffocating). When a blight struck the Atlantic Eelgrass beds in 1931, the scallop fishery was adversely affected. Since then, both Eelgrass and Bay Scallops have recovered in population.

The Calico Scallop is similar in shape and size to the Bay Scallop. The calico name arises from markings on the upper shell: irregular blotches or stripes of a "calico" nature. The Calico Scallop, too, is fished commercially, but offshore in deeper water.

The Sea Scallop is found mainly above Cape Hatteras in North Carolina. A larger species, the Sea Scallop shell reaches eight inches in length. Like the Calico Scallop, it is fished commercially offshore.

Scallops are found on the beach in a wide array of colors. Bright oranges and reds are especially visible when the shells are wet. Some beached shells are dark, with colors ranging from gray to brown or even black; these darker shells have been buried in offshore muck, and part of the calcium carbonate in the shells has been replaced with iron sulfide.

Scallops are highly prized by man as food. The attractive, white meat has a rich, almost sweet flavor. Interestingly, the only part of a scallop eaten in the U.S. is the single adductor muscle (the part that holds the shells together). In European countries, the whole animal is eaten.

Rumors abound that restaurants cut plugs of meat from skates or sharks, passing it off as scallops. This practice is probably very rare. One way to distinguish scallop meat is to gently pull the morsels apart — scallop meat separates easily, and all the fibers run in one direction.

SCOTCH BONNET
picture 57

The Scotch Bonnet is a prized find to Carolina shell collectors. The design of the shell is unique, and it is an uncommon specimen on the beach. Also, it is the official state seashell of North Carolina.

In size, the Scotch Bonnet ranges up to four inches. The underlying white color is highlighted by distinct rows of reddish-brown spots circling the shell. Ridges, set off by grooves, also circle the shell. The top of the  roughly egg-shaped shell is a pointed spire. The shell opening is large, and the thick outer lip is toothed. At the bottom of the shell, the lips meet and turn upward to form a small groove.

A snail-like animal (gastropod) lives inside the shell. Like most snails, it has tentacles which are tactile organs. The shell is also a favorite home of hermit crabs, so the animal inside the shell may not be the original occupant!

Scotch Bonnets live in deep water offshore. Rough seas sometimes push Bonnets into shallow water. In fact, a powerful surf can wash the heavy shells onto the beach (the best time to find Scotch Bonnets on the beach is after a storm). The shell is often faded when found on shore, but the sculpture is intact.

The prey of Scotch Bonnets includes sand dollars and sea urchins. Bonnets secrete a substance containing sulfuric acid to dissolve the outer tests (shells) of these animals. After an opening is made in the shell, the inner edible flesh is eaten.

The Scotch Bonnet is a member of the helmet shell family. Larger members of this family are used as signal horns in the Tropics.

In May, 1965, the North Carolina General Assembly designated the Scotch Bonnet as the official state seashell of North Carolina. This marked the first time a state named an official seashell.

SLIPPER SHELL
picture 58

Slipper shells are small ovals, usually less than two inches long. The characteristic feature of a slipper shell is a shelf inside the shell (diagram 17); the shells thus resemble a small slipper or boat, and so the common names slipper shell and boat shell.

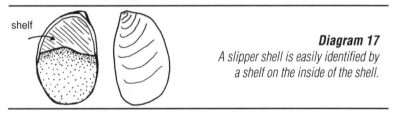

shelf

Diagram 17
A slipper shell is easily identified by a shelf on the inside of the shell.

The Common Atlantic Slipper shell is the species most often found on our seashore. It is white, with irregular brown stripes or splotches. The shell has a white shelf, covering one-third to one-half of the opening.

At first glance, a slipper shell would appear to house a clam-like animal having two shells (bivalve). Rather, the animal lives in a single shell; it is a gastropod, a snail-like animal (one of very few marine snails that form shells not coiled in a spiral shape). The shelf inside the shell serves to protect and support the snail.

The gastropod attaches to hard objects with its large foot and remains still most of the time. It may attach to rocks, Horseshoe Crabs, hermit crab shells, other shells such as oysters, or even to other slipper shells.

Although slipper shells often live attached to other animals, they do not feed on their hosts. Instead, slipper shells filter plankton from sea water (thus, slipper shells not only resemble bivalves, they also feed like them).

Slipper shells are hermaphroditic (organs of both sexes are present in each individual). The male and female sexual organs operate at different

61

times of the spawning season or life of the animal, preventing self-fertilization. In general, the younger, more active snails are males. They become female later in life and are more sedentary.

Although slipper shells do not feed on oysters, they can be harmful to them; slipper shells sometimes grow on top of oyster beds to the extent that they crowd out the oysters.

SUNDIAL

picture 59

Sundial shells are small spirals, measuring less than two inches wide. They are circular, flattened, and, indeed, resemble small sundials.

The Common Sundial shell is white, with raised spiral ridges on its top and bottom. Brown spots on the ridges form brown spiral lines. There are two openings on the bottom of the shell. The larger opening leads to the interior of the shell, where the snail-like animal resides. The smaller opening is a deep umbilicus, or "belly button," around which the whorls of the shell are formed.

SURF CLAM

picture 60

Shells of the Surf Clam are rather common on Carolina beaches. Specimens south of Cape Hatteras, however, are generally smaller than in northern states.

Compared to a Quahog Clam Shell, the Surf Clam is thinner-shelled, and the umbo (bulge at the hinge) is central, not pushed to one side.

The shape of the Surf Clam shell can be described as an oval triangle. These shells are often mistaken as tellins, another group of shells which they resemble.

The shell of larger specimens is gray-white on the outside, white to cream on the inside. Smaller shells are tan-brown on the outside, lighter tan on the inside. Part of the tan coloration is due to the periostracum, the thin covering on the outside of the shell. Some of the color is due to pigment within the shell, acquired from sediment where the clam lives.

The outside of a Surf Clam shell is smooth, but fine concentric growth lines are visible.

On the inside of a Surf Clam shell, a faint white chalky area where the mantle attaches is easily seen. Looking closely at the hinge region, a triangular depression where the ligament inserts is visible. Two small grooved wings extend from either side of this depression.

The Surf Clam is avidly sought commercially from New England to Virginia. Larger specimens (up to seven inches) occur in offshore beds in water up to 140 feet deep. The clams are dredged from the bottom by boat.

Like scallops, only the adductor muscles of the clam are used as food. Surf Clams are often cooked and eaten as clam strips.

Seventy percent of the clams taken commercially in the U.S. are Surf Clams. The smaller size of specimens south of Cape Hatteras, however, makes Surf Clams commercially less important here.

Other names for the Surf Clam include Atlantic Surf Clam, Beach Clam, and Skimmer Clam.

Like other bivalves, the Surf Clam lives buried just beneath the ocean bottom. The mollusk extends short siphons above the surface to bring in water; food and oxygen are extracted from sea water via the incurrent siphon, and wastes are expelled by the excurrent siphon.

TULIP SHELL

picture 61

Tulip shells have a characteristic spiral shape, pointed at both ends. The ivory color of the shell is offset by brown or tan splotches. Tulips are also distinguished by their large size and thin brown lines which spiral around the outside of the shell.

Two species of tulip shells are found in the Carolinas, the Banded Tulip and True Tulip. The Banded Tulip is fairly common; it reaches four and one-half inches in length. The Banded Tulip has seven thin, distinct brown lines on its main whorl, and the sutures between its whorls are smooth. The True Tulip is less common; it grows much larger, to nine or ten inches in length. The True Tulip has more than 15 faint brown lines on its main whorl, and the sutures between its whorls are rough.

Black, snail-like animals reside in and form tulip shells. When picked up or threatened by a predator, a tulip snail retreats into its shell and seals the opening with a lid-like covering (operculum).

Tulip snails are carnivorous, preying on other large gastropods and mollusks. Using a tongue-like radula, they bore a hole through the shell of a snail or clam and eat the inhabitant. Tulip shells are also cannibalistic, readily consuming other tulip shells. The Banded Tulip is edible; it tastes much like whelk or conch.

TURKEY WING

picture 62

The distinct shape and pattern of a Turkey Wing shell make it easily recognizable. The shape is roughly rectangular; the color pattern is white, highlighted by wavy brown lines.

The shape and pattern of the shell do, indeed, bring to mind a turkey's wing. The wavy brown lines also resemble lines on a zebra, giving it the nickname "Zebra Ark Shell."

Turkey Wing shells usually measure close to two inches but range up to four inches in length. In addition to the distinct wavy lines, raised ribs extend in a fan-like pattern from the hinge. The lip of the shell on the hinge side is remarkably straight and marked with very fine teeth.

The live Turkey Wing is a bivalve mollusk; its two shells are covered with a brown, shaggy outer coat. These animals live attached to rocks, coral, and other shells; they anchor themselves to these substrates by tough, thin strands called byssal threads. In some areas of the Caribbean and South America, Turkey Wings are eaten by man.

WHELKS
picture 63

Whelks are very evident on Carolina beaches: Both the shells and egg cases of whelks are commonly seen.

"Big, ocean-going snails" is an apt description of whelks. Whelk shells are large, measuring up to 12 inches long. They are roughly pear-shaped; the top is wide, with a short spire on top, and the bottom tapers gradually.

Three whelks are common to the Carolinas; they are easily identified and distinguished (diagram 18).

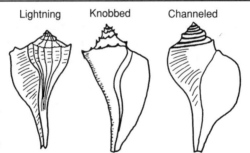

Lightning   Knobbed   Channeled

Diagram 18
The three most common whelks of the Carolina coast are easily identified. The Lightning Whelk opens to the left. The Knobbed Whelk exhibits knobs on the spire. The Channeled Whelk has grooves on the spire.

To identify a whelk shell, hold it with the opening facing you, spire on top, thin neck down. The LIGHTNING WHELK is the only one that **opens to the left** (easy to remember: L in lightning and left). The CHANNELED WHELK has distinct grooves or **channels between the whorls** on the top of the shell; it opens to the right, has a rounder opening, and has a fuzzy periostracum when alive. The KNOBBED WHELK has **definite knobs on its spire**, and it also opens to the right. The Knobbed Whelk has an orange aperture as well.

Classified as gastropods (single shell, broad foot), whelks prey upon bivalves (clams, oysters, mussels, etc.). To eat a clam, a whelk grasps it with its strong, muscular foot. The whelk then wedges the lip of its shell between the two shells of the clam, and attempts to pry it apart. If successful in opening the clam shell just a crack, a whelk can get enough of its snail-like head inside to begin eating the mollusk.

Though whelks are carnivorous (meat eating), preying mainly upon live bivalves, they also eat carrion (dead, decaying flesh). Channeled Whelks are especially prone to seek carrion: They are often caught in crab traps, feeding on the bait.

Hermit crabs are often found in whelk shells, as they are one of the crabs' favorite shells to inhabit.

Like conchs found in tropical waters, whelks are utilized in several ways. Whelk shells can be used as signal horns. Whelk meat is excellent in chowder and is quite tasty in salsa dishes. Whelk meat can, in fact, be substituted in any recipe calling for clams.

The egg cases of whelks are also found on the beach. Egg capsules of the Knobbed Whelk are square-edged, while egg capsules of the Channeled Whelk are sharp-edged (see section on whelk egg cases, page 104).

WORM SHELL
picture 64

Worm Shells are small tubular shells, typically amber in color. The first part of the shell is a tightly-coiled spiral; the distal shell is loosely coiled and more variable in form.

Despite the worm-like shape of its shell, the animal living in the shell is a gastropod, a snail-like mollusk. The snail lives alone, not in colonies like other worm shell species. The Worm Shell often attaches to other shells, rocks, or live sponges.

Another name for the Worm Shell is Old Maid's Curl.

Flounder begin life like other fish— upright, with eyes on opposite sides of the head. Gradually, they begin listing to one side, and one eye migrates to the "top" side. They spend the rest of their life sideways, swimming and lying flat on the bottom.

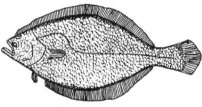

FISH

Fish are the dominant group of larger animals in the ocean. Besides being aquatic, fish are characterized as being cold-blooded vertebrates, possessing gills for breathing and fins for swimming.

Marine fish have adapted to virtually every niche and habitat in the ocean; as a result, species vary greatly in size, shape, features, and behavior.

Fish swim by using extensive body muscle groups in an organized fashion, pushing water backward and their bodies forward. The muscles are what humans eat when consuming a meal of fish.

The fins of a fish are both paired and unpaired. Paired fins (diagram 19) include the pectorals and pelvics. Unpaired fins consist of the dorsal, anal, and caudal (tail) fins. Normally, only the tail fin is used for propulsion; the other fins are used in turning, braking, and fine movements.

The lateral line is a unique sensory system of fish. This sense organ consists of a row of pores that are connected by a canal running just below the body surface. This system enables a fish to "feel at a distance"; by

Diagram 19
The pectoral and pelvic fins of a fish are paired. The dorsal, tail (caudal), and anal fins are unpaired.

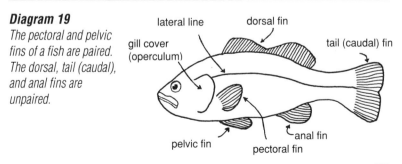

detecting pressure differences in the water, a fish is able to sense objects and movement.

The teeth of a fish vary in size, shape, and location, depending on what the fish eats; teeth may be located on the jaws, tongue, roof of the mouth, or pharynx (throat).

Some fish have barbels located under the mouth, used for feeling and tasting.

Interestingly, fish continue to grow until they die; they do not reach adult size and cease growing like most other animals.

Many marine fish are OSEND, or Ocean-Spawned, Estuarine-Nursery Dependent. Mature female fish lay eggs offshore. The free-floating eggs hatch into tiny larvae, which can move about on their own to some extent but are largely dependent on currents, tides, and winds for large-scale travel. These forces usually act to sweep the larvae into estuaries. The tiny fish spend several months in the estuarine marshes, finding food for growth and protection from predators. Only after this initial period of marsh nurturing do the fish venture forth into sound and ocean waters.

Fish can be divided into two main groups: bony fish and cartilaginous fish. The bony group of marine fish is the most abundant and widespread; about 90 percent of fish species possess skeletons composed of bone. Most of the other 10 percent of marine fish are in the cartilaginous group, with skeletons composed of cartilage.

Bony fish can be distinguished from cartilaginous fish at a glance: The presence of a gill cover identifies a bony fish. The gill cover, or operculum, is a semicircular flap behind the fish's head.

Bony fish also possess a swim bladder, an important and unique structure which cartilaginous fish lack. The swim bladder is a gas-filled internal sac; it enables a fish to maintain neutral buoyancy in the water. A bony fish remains weightless in the water by increasing or decreasing the amount of gas in its swim bladder; a bony fish does not sink to the bottom, even if it ceases swimming. A scuba diver uses a device called a buoyancy compensator just like a fish uses its swim bladder: By varying the amount of gas in an external sac, the diver maintains neutral buoyancy.

Cartilaginous fish (sharks, rays, and skates), despite their lesser numbers, include some of the most successful predators in the ocean. Instead of a gill cover, cartilaginous fish possess five to seven gill slits (diagram 20). Unlike bony fish, they must keep swimming, or they will sink to the bottom.

Bony and cartilaginous fish differ in other ways as well. Cartilaginous fish reproduce by internal fertilization; some species even bear live young. Bony fish reproduce by a less-complicated method of external fertilization. Cartilaginous fish, for the most part, lack cone cells in their eyes, so they cannot see colors; not surprisingly, sharks, rays, and skates are typically

Diagram 20
Cartilaginous fish (sharks, rays, and skates) have gill slits.

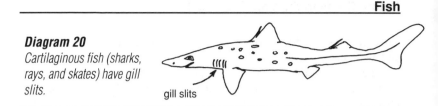

gill slits

drab in color. Bony fish, having cone cells, can perceive color; the colors of bony fish are more varied and vivid.

Scales cover the skin of most fish. Along with a mucus layer, scales function to protect a fish and prevent it from drying out. Sharks have tooth-like dermal scales which give their skin a rough, sandpaper-like texture. Bony fish typically have flat, round scales, marked by rings called circuli; circuli provide a rough estimate of the age of a fish (similar to rings on a tree).

The salinity of a fish's body is midway between that of fresh water and ocean water. A fish must compensate, as it constantly loses fresh water through its skin by osmosis. Bony fish compensate by drinking seawater, then excreting salt through their gills and intestine. Sharks, skates, and rays prevent water loss by retaining the waste product urea in their blood; urea balances the animal osmotically.

Many skates, rays, and sharks possess spiracles. Spiracles consist of an outer opening, usually behind the eye, connected by a tube to the gills. Water enters the spiracle opening, then flows over the gills, where oxygen is extracted. Spiracles thus serve as an accessory mouth in providing water for breathing (nostrils in fish serve for smell, not for breathing). Spiracles are found in species that lie and feed on the bottom. These species often have mouths on their underside; while resting on the bottom, the fish can't take in water by mouth as well.

A myriad of fish species occur in Carolina waters — truly a wonder of biologic diversity. The species most often seen by coastal residents and visitors are discussed in the following sections.

BLUEFISH
picture 65

Bluefish are a popular catch among Carolina surf anglers. They provide both a good fight and a tasty meal. Usually, Blues weigh from one to twelve pounds; the record Blue caught in North Carolina is 31 pounds, in South Carolina, 21 pounds. Bluefish can live as long as 14 years.

Bluefish have a "gamefish" appearance. They have a long shape, big head, and large jaw with obvious sharp teeth. Their color is silver, with a blue-green tinge.

Like mackerel, Bluefish make seasonal migrations along the East Coast. Traveling in schools of similarly-sized fish, Blues head north in warmer weather, south in colder weather. As they prefer water in the 66 to 72 degree range, Blues are more commonly caught in inshore Carolina waters in the spring and fall.

The feeding behavior of Bluefish is remarkable. They are voracious predators, attacking schools of fish, squid, and marine worms. Menhaden and mullet provide much of their food. Bluefish swim through fish schools, slashing to and fro with their teeth. Often, they kill far more than they can eat. Bluefish are also cannibalistic — they eat smaller fish of their own species (one reason why Blues swimming in the same school are all close in size).

Bluefish can eat twice their weight each day. Some sources report that Bluefish gorge until full, regurgitate, then feed again. This "Roman orgy" behavior probably does not occur in nature, though Bluefish sometimes regurgitate bait fish when caught.

When "the Blues are running," they strike at anything resembling a small fish. Surf fishermen have a field day pulling them in. Anglers must be careful wading when Blues are in a feeding frenzy: Blues have been known to inflict multiple cuts on waders and swimmers.

Sharp teeth line a Bluefish's mouth in a single row. As the teeth can inflict a deep cut even after landed, Bluefish must be handled with care.

Bluefish have a strong flavor; they are best when eaten fresh. The flavor of Blues can also be optimized by bleeding and icing the fish immediately after catching.

BURRFISH / PUFFER
pictures 66, 67, 68

Burrfish and puffers are very similar fish that exhibit a most unusual behavior. When threatened, these fish quickly inflate their bellies with water, achieving a larger size and globular shape. The sudden change in body size and configuration discourages predators from attempting to swallow them.

Several species of both burrfish and puffers are found in Carolina waters. In addition, burrfish are often called puffers because of their similar bloating behavior, and both groups of fish have several nicknames, including blowfish, swell toad, blow toad, and swellfish.

Several anatomical features are shared by burrfish and puffers. Both fish are small, reaching only about ten inches in length. Pelvic fins are absent. Other fins are soft (without stiff rays) and located far back on the body. Gill openings are reduced to small slits. Teeth are absent; in place of teeth, jaw bones are adapted to form sharp-edged plates.

Both burrfish and puffers use their beak-like jaw plates to crush hard-shelled animals such as mollusks, crustaceans, and sea urchins. The jaw plates of the burrfish are solid, without interruption. The puffer, on the other hand, has a gap in the midline of its jaw plates, so the plates resemble buck teeth.

An expandable extension of the stomach enables burrfish and puffers to distend with water. The fish also have scaleless, elastic skin, which stretches easily. If burrfish or puffers are removed from water (such as when landed by a fisherman), they bloat with air.

Burrfish can be distinguished from puffers by very obvious rigid spines on their body. Puffers have much smaller bumps, not visible at a glance; the bumps give puffers' skin a rough texture. While both fish are odd-shaped, the body forms of the fish differ. Burrfish are shaped like a thick loaf of bread, while puffers are more slender, like a hot dog bun.

Burrfish and puffers are usually caught in the surf or in sounds. A fisherman must be an expert to eat these fish. The flesh of burrfish can be poisonous. Also, some species of puffers are highly toxic; others are toxic in just part of their living range. If puffers are cleaned properly, avoiding toxin concentrated in the gallbladder, the reward is ample; the meat of the Northern Puffer, marketed as "sea squab" or "chicken of the sea," tastes like a cross between chicken and fish.

Puffers are commonly eaten in Japan, where chefs must be certified in puffer cleaning and preparation. There, despite the chefs' careful efforts, puffer toxin causes several fatalities each year.

Locomotion in burrfish and puffers is relatively slow; the fish do not swim as most fish (with powerful movements of the tail fin). Instead, burrfish and puffers move by rapidly fanning their small pectoral, dorsal, and anal fins; this fin fluttering gives the fish an even more unique appearance.

The odd shape, unusual bloating behavior, atypical swimming motion, and general hardiness of burrfish and puffers make them good aquarium fish.

CROAKER

picture 69

The Atlantic Croaker is a commonly-caught species on the Carolina coast.

Croaker are typically small fish, one-fourth to one pound in size; the record in North Carolina is five pounds, in South Carolina, four and a half pounds.

The coloration of a Croaker is silver-green on top and white-to-yellow below. A pattern of slender, oblique bars marks the top half of the body. The pectoral and tail fins are often a golden yellow. A black marking appears at the base of the pectoral fin.

The mouth of a Croaker is set low on its head. The Croaker's tail fin is somewhat unique in shape; the middle sticks outward, giving it a convex shape (unlike the concave-shaped caudal fin on most fish). Other characteristics of a Croaker include a green iris, a spotted dorsal fin, and four barbels on each side of the lower jaw. During spawning season, the lower half of a Croaker's body may turn golden, and the fish are marketed as "Golden Croaker."

Croaker, like Spot, kingfish, and Red Drum, are members of the drum family; these fish make drumming sounds using pharyngeal teeth and special muscles on the wall of their swim bladder. The low croaking noise Croakers make after they are caught gives them their name.

In warmer weather, Croaker are caught in shallow, brackish water of bays and estuaries. During the colder part of the year, Croakers move offshore to deeper water. Croakers are bottom dwellers, feeding on a varied diet of shrimp, mollusks, worms, crustaceans, and detritus.

The varied diet of Croakers is one reason they are so widespread and successful. Also, Croaker tolerate a wide range of water temperature and salinity, and they thrive in both muddy and sandy-bottom habitats.

Croakers are a popular food species; they are easy to catch, clean, and cook. They are most often pan-fried but can be broiled, baked, or poached. The lean white meat of Croakers is quite tasty. The meat, like that of snook and cobia, is white even when raw.

EEL
picture 70

The American Eel is a snakelike, slimy-skinned fish. It is frequently caught in coastal Carolina waters, where it averages eight to sixteen inches in length.

Like other eels, the American Eel is a true bony fish, possessing both a bony skeleton and jaws. It is far removed from the primitive Lamprey Eel, which is not a true eel at all; Lampreys are very primitive fish with no jaws.

The American Eel is unmistakable in appearance. The fish is long, cylindrical, and green (longer specimens are gray). The head narrows to a point, and thick lips are prominent. The Eel has a wavy, prominent fin on the back half of its body; the fin is continuous on the top and bottom of the eel, wrapping around its pointed tail (the dorsal, tail, and anal fins are joined into one long fin). When caught and laid on a solid surface, an Eel exhibits a characteristic winding, sinuous motion and oozes a white mucus from its body.

The life cycle of the American Eel is interesting. The Eel is a catadromous fish, meaning it is a freshwater fish that migrates to the ocean to spawn. An American Eel may migrate hundreds or even thousands of miles from its home river to breed!

Newborn Eels hatch and begin their lives in the Sargasso Sea, a part of the Atlantic Ocean southeast of Bermuda (diagram 21). Larval Eels, vastly different in form from adults, spend their first year in these warm waters.

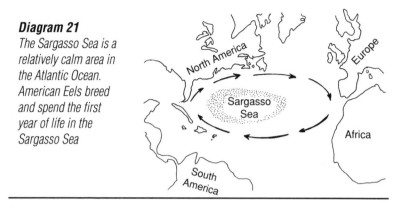

Diagram 21
The Sargasso Sea is a relatively calm area in the Atlantic Ocean. American Eels breed and spend the first year of life in the Sargasso Sea

In their second year, young Eels travel to the North American coast; their destination extends from Labrador to Florida. At this time, they are about three inches long, flat, colorless, and leaflike. These larval forms subsequently metamorphose into elvers, which are round, transparent, and have the adult Eel shape.

Elvers enter fresh water, where they take on the green-brown color of adults. The elvers migrate up rivers, often far inland, where they mature into adult Eels. Males remain in fresh water five to twelve years, growing up to three feet in length. Females remain 10 to 24 years, growing up to five feet in length.

After spending most of their lives in fresh water, adult Eels journey back to their breeding grounds in the Sargasso Sea. It is mostly during this downstream spawning run that they are caught by commercial and recreational fishermen. The adult Eels will never again return to fresh water, since they die after breeding.

Wire mesh pots are used to catch American Eels commercially. The market for Eel meat in the U.S. is fairly small. However, a significant market for Eel exists in the Orient and Europe; in both places, the white flesh is considered a delicacy. Eel may sell in foreign markets for five to ten times what it sells for in the U.S.

If a Carolinian is willing to ignore Eels' snakelike, slimy, squirming appearance, and further willing to pull off Eels' tough skin, there is ample reward. Eel meat is quite good either fried or smoked.

Eels do serve another function locally; they are often used as live bait for larger game fish.

FLOUNDER

picture 71

Flounder, like halibut, fluke, turbot, and sole, are flatfish; their bodies are flattened into an oval pancake shape. The underside of flounders is white; on top, they are brown, with darker spots and splotches.

The flat shape and color of flounder enable them to blend with the bottom where they live. Their color actually changes to match different bottoms. Flounders' camouflage serves two functions: 1) Flounder escape detection by predators, and 2) flounder remain unseen by their own prey (shrimp, small fish, and crabs) until the animals are close enough to be caught.

Several species of flounder are caught in the Carolinas; three species are common. Summer Flounder have five distinct ocellated (eye-like) dark spots on their brown topside, while Gulf Flounder have three distinct ocellated spots. The Southern Flounder, the most common species, has indistinct spots and blotches but lacks the distinct ocellated spots of its cousins.

Most flounder caught here weigh less than five pounds; the record for North Carolina is 20 1/2 pounds, in South Carolina, 17 1/2 pounds.

During warm weather, flounder move inshore. Smaller flounder come all the way into shallow tidal flats to feed. There, they can be caught with hook and line, or gigged with a spear, using a light to spot them on the bottom at night.

Interestingly, flounder are sideways-oriented. Some flat fish, such as rays and skates, lie with their belly on the bottom. Flounder, though, actually lie and swim on their side!

When a flounder hatches, the larval flounder is oriented like other fish. Shortly thereafter, it begins listing to one side when swimming. Then, one of the flounder's eyes literally migrates to its other side. The side with two eyes then becomes the "top" of the fish, and the side without eyes, the "bottom." The flounder spends the rest of its life in this sideways orientation; whether the right or left side is down depends on the species of flounder.

A flounder also loses its swim bladder as it changes to a sideways orientation. An adult flounder thus shares several characteristics with skates and rays: flat pancake shape, bottom dwelling, and lack of an air bladder.

The diet of a flounder is varied and includes shrimp, small fish, crabs, and squid. A flounder feeds by stealth: Natural camouflage is augmented by partial burying in the sand; the flounder remains still and unseen until prey ventures near, then a sudden dash is made to snare prey.

Flounder are caught by sport and commercial fishermen alike. They are prized for their excellent taste; whether broiled, baked, or fried, flounder is one of the best tasting fish anywhere.

KINGFISH (WHITING)

picture 72

Kingfish are often caught while surf fishing, as they frequent shallow water along beaches. Kingfish are known by other names in various locales, including whiting, Virginia mullet, and sea mullet.

The shape of kingfish is long and slender; the color is silvery. The kingfish's mouth is set low on its head. A single, short barbel is present on the chin. The second dorsal fin is long, and the tail fin is asymmetrical, with the top half pointed, the bottom half rounded.

Three species of kingfish occur in Carolina coastal waters: The Southern Kingfish is by far the most common; it is distinguished by seven or eight indistinct, dark, diagonal bars on each side. Gulf Kingfish lack the dark bars; the tip of the first dorsal fin is dark. Northern Kingfish are darker overall, and exhibit five or six well-defined, dark bars on the side. Northern Kingfish also have a long spine on the first dorsal fin.

Like Spot, Croaker, and Red Drum, kingfish are members of the drum family. They are bottom dwellers; kingfish use their chin barbel to probe the bottom for worms, crabs, and shrimp.

Kingfish can reach 18 inches and weigh two and a half pounds. They make excellent eating, especially if fresh. The taste of kingfish, like the taste of Bluefish, is not as good after freezing.

LIZARD FISH

picture 73

The Lizard Fish is aptly named; its long, slender form and wide, gaping jaws make it lizard-like in appearance.

Also known as the Inshore Lizardfish, this species is marked by a pattern of eight dark diamond shapes on its side. Typically running six to eight inches in length, Lizard Fish can grow to 18 inches long.

Many small teeth line the large mouth of the Lizard Fish. A voracious predator, the Lizard Fish feeds on smaller fish and shrimp.

The Lizard Fish is a bottom dweller, preferring eelgrass beds on sandy bottoms. It can burrow in loose bottom sediment to hide.

Anglers catch Lizard Fish more often than they like, as most fishermen consider them a nuisance. The Lizard Fish is not usually eaten, though they are relished in Southeast Asia.

If one is brave enough to sample a Lizard Fish, the taste is surprisingly good. The flesh does contain tiny bones, which must be picked out or chewed up while eating the fish. Before scoffing at the idea of chewing up small bones in a piece of fish, remember: Salmon meat has similar bones, and is it ever expensive!

MACKEREL
picture 74

Mackerel are large, highly-sought-after game fish. They are valuable to commercial and recreational fishermen alike. Several "King Mackerel" tournaments are held all along the Carolina coast each year; the tournaments attract fishermen from all over the Carolinas.

Two species of mackerel are commonly caught in the Carolinas: King Mackerel and Spanish Mackerel. The main difference between the species is size: Spanish Mackerel are smaller.

Both mackerel species are blue on top, silver below. Rows of rather unique dorsal and anal finlets on the back one-third of the body distinguish mackerel from most other fish. The long, sleek shape and deeply forked (lunate) tail of mackerel enable them to swim very swiftly.

The larger of the two species, King Mackerel, grow up to 79 pounds in the Carolinas. Larger King Mackerel can be told from Spanish Mackerel by the absence of yellow spots on their bodies. Smaller Kings, like Spanish, have many round yellow body spots, which fade rapidly after death. Smaller King Mackerel are thus often confused with Spanish Mackerel. Smaller Kings can be distinguished from Spanish by two obvious characteristics: Kings have a lateral line turning downward sharply (diagram 22), and the front part of the spinous dorsal fin is clear (no pigment). "Kings are clearly down" is a good mnemonic to remember the characteristics.

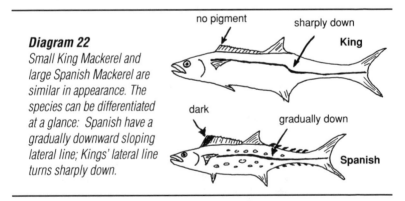

Diagram 22
Small King Mackerel and large Spanish Mackerel are similar in appearance. The species can be differentiated at a glance: Spanish have a gradually downward sloping lateral line; Kings' lateral line turns sharply down.

no pigment
sharply down
King
dark
gradually down
Spanish

Spanish Mackerel, the smaller species, average two to three pounds, but range up to 13 pounds in the Carolinas. Although pelagic (ocean-going) like Kings, Spanish are also found and caught in bays. Both small and large Spanish have bright yellow spots on their blue-silver bodies. Characteristics which distinguish Spanish from small King Mackerel include a lateral line that slopes more evenly downward and a dark area on the first six spines of the dorsal fin (diagram 22, *picture 74*).

Both mackerel species prefer warm water, 68 degrees or above. As a result, both species migrate south in the fall and winter.

The size and speed of mackerel allow them to move through schools of Menhaden and other small fish in "feeding frenzies." The mackerel eat some fish whole, but only parts of others, and leave many dead fish in the water.

Mackerel are highly regarded as food. Spanish and smaller Kings can be filleted. Larger fish are often cut into one- to two-inch sections and served as "steaks."

Because mackerel are highly desired game fish, and because modern technology (larger nets, loran, depth finders) enables man to catch more mackerel, mackerel populations are dwindling. Presently, regulations controlling mackerel catches vary from state to state, and a more equitable plan covering all mackerel-inhabited waters may be necessary to protect these species.

MENHADEN
picture 75

Menhaden, also known as "pogy" or "fatbacks," are small fish, ordinary in appearance. They are brown on top, silvery below; the fins are yellowish. A Menhaden's mouth is large; the lower jaw fits neatly into a notch in the upper jaw. There is a distinct black spot behind a Menhaden's head and frequently other spots on its sides.

Usually, Menhaden travel in schools. The fish average six to eight inches in length; they can grow to 18 inches, living up to ten years.

Menhaden are oily fish, making them unpalatable for man.

Despite their common appearance, small size, and undesirable taste, Menhaden are a very important species.

First, Menhaden are sought by commercial fishermen. Menhaden boats drag huge nets, catching hundreds of thousands of schooling Menhaden. Fish oil is the main product of Menhaden processing; the oil is used to make paints and cosmetics. Other parts of the fish are ground up to make animal meal and fertilizer.

Occasionally, a net on a Menhaden boat breaks, releasing huge numbers of dead fish. If the fish wash up on a beach, it creates a great stink (literally and politically). Coastal tourism suffers until the dead Menhaden are cleaned up.

Although important commercially, Menhaden are of much greater importance as an essential link in ocean food chains. The diet of Menhaden consists of plankton (microscopic plants and animals that are the basic producers of the oceans). Menhaden, in turn, are eaten by numerous other animals including tuna, bluefish, cod, sharks, other fish, whales, dolphins, squid, gulls, terns, osprey, and pelicans. Suffice it to say that Menhaden are a key ingredient in many animals' diets; they are the link between plankton producers and flesh-eating predators.

Menhaden are successful and prolific enough to serve as a food source for larger animals because they possess a highly-efficient and unique feeding mechanism. The gills of Menhaden function not only as breathing organs, but also as feeding appendages. Specialized feeding parts of the gills called gillrakers filter plankton as the fish swim through water.

In this manner, a Menhaden can filter six to seven gallons of seawater a minute and extract one pint of food an hour! Although toothless, unable to chew even a bite of food, a Menhaden can grow to six inches long in its first year.

For protection, Menhaden travel in huge schools numbering in the hundreds of thousands. Schools migrate along the coast, heading north as waters warm, and south again as waters cool. The fish swim near the surface of the water, where they are often seen rippling the surface.

The rippling of surface water is one sign that alerts sport and commercial fishermen to the presence of Menhaden. Sport fishermen also seek Menhaden — for bait; fishermen throw a small round cast net over the schooling fish to catch them. The netted Menhaden are kept alive in bait wells on board the fishing boats. Using Menhaden to "live bait" fish for King Mackerel is very successful along the Carolina coast.

MULLET
picture 76

Mullet are silvery fish, with a blue-green tinge. The shape of mullet is tubular; they have a rounded head and a small mouth. The pectoral fins of mullet are set higher than on most fish. The scales of mullet are large and round, and mullet lack a lateral line on the body.

Several species of mullet exist in coastal Carolina waters. The Striped Mullet is by far and away the most important, however. Striped Mullet are marked by six or seven dark stripes running lengthwise on their sides. Most specimens are 8 to 18 inches in size, but Striped Mullet can reach 24 inches in length.

Mullet travel in large schools. They venture from the open ocean into estuaries and even into fresh-water rivers. Mullet are often seen leaping out of the water. The exact reason mullet jump clear of the water is not known; jumping to escape from predators seems to explain only part of the leaping behavior.

Mullet feed on muddy bottoms; they consume algae, green plants, and small animals. Food is often obtained directly from mud. Mullet suck mud into their mouth; a sifting mechanism on their gillrakers separates food particles and waste matter from mud.

Striped Mullet spawn offshore in the fall, and the eggs are carried into estuaries by currents and waves. After hatching, juvenile Mullet remain in the estuaries six to eight months. The Striped Mullet fingerlings are often netted by fishermen, as they make excellent bait for larger game fish.

Commercial fishermen seek mullet in offshore waters. Nets are used to catch mullet — being largely herbivorous, the fish rarely take a baited hook. Many of the netted mullet are used for food; often, they are smoked. Fresh mullet is also quite acceptable if broiled, baked, barbecued, or fried.

The roe (eggs) of mullet is also considered a delicacy by some Carolinians; in Japan, mullet roe may sell for over $50 a pound!

Another use of mullet is as fish bait: cut bait for rod and reel angling, live bait for flounder, bluefish, mackerel, and trout.

Mullet are most important, though, as a source of food for other animals. Many animals feed on schools of mullet, including countless larger fish, many birds, and dolphins. Like Menhaden, mullet provide an enormous, crucial link in oceanic food chains.

OYSTER TOADFISH
picture 77

Oyster Toadfish, or "Mud Toads," are not a popular catch among fishermen; they are often landed while fishing for other species of fish. Also, they must be handled with care to safely get them off the hook. Nevertheless, Oyster Toads are a common catch in the Carolinas. As a matter of fact, there are some "Toadfish-King Fishermen" who seem to catch nothing else. It is in honor of these luckless anglers that the following discussion is given.

The appearance of the Oyster Toad is drab, almost grotesque. Toadfish are dark brown in color. The skin is scaleless, wrinkled, and covered with a slimy mucus. Toadfish have a large head and jaws. Small, fleshy growths protrude from the head and mouth area, and bulging eyes are set on top of the flat head. The Toadfish's dorsal fin is long and wavy; the pectoral fins (behind the gills) are large, fan-shaped, and marked by concentric dark bands. The maximum length of the fish is about 15 inches.

When landed and out of water, an Oyster Toad opens its large mouth very wide, as if gasping. It may grunt loudly when handled (as it does while hunting in the water at night). Male Toadfish are also said to make a sound like a boat whistle during spawing season, using the noise to attract females.

Toadfish must be handled carefully for two reasons: 1) Their strong jaws can inflict a painful bite, and 2) toadfish have hard-to-see, stiff spines in their fins; these spines can inflict a puncture wound which is painful and prone to infection.

Despite its unattractive appearance, danger in handling, and lackluster reputation, the Toadfish is edible. Apparently, a fisherman must be both hungry and careful to enjoy the taste of one.

The Oyster Toad is a bottom-dwelling fish, living in shallow water, especially in rocky or weedy areas. There, they hunt for a wide variety of animals including crabs, anemones, clams, shrimp, sea urchins, and small fish. Toadfish also eat some vegetation.

The reproductive behavior of the Oyster Toad is remarkable. The female lays her eggs in a cavity or under debris, near the low tide mark. The male Toadfish then guards the nest while the eggs are incubating, about three weeks. He keeps silt off the eggs and defends the nest against predators. The male Toadfish's protective instinct is so strong that he is sometimes left high and dry when an unusually low tide leaves the nest out of the water. In view of this valorous behavior, perhaps the Toadfish deserves to be held in higher esteem!

PIGFISH
picture 78

Pigfish are small fish, frequently caught in the inshore waters of the Carolinas.

Typically, Pigfish weigh about one-half pound and are six to eight inches in length; they can grow to weigh three pounds and measure 18 inches. Pigfish have a blue-gray body, with characteristic bronze-to-orange spots or dashes. The mouth of a Pigfish is small, set more inferiorly on the head than the mouth is set on a Pinfish. Pigfish are members of the grunt family.

Pigfish and Pinfish share many characteristics. Both are small, frequently-caught panfish. Pigfish and Pinfish are underutilized as food: One reason is their names. If Pigfish and Pinfish were re-named Orange-Spotted Perch and Spot Perch, respectively, they would find a solid niche in the seafood market.

Although small, Pigfish are quite tasty. One need only take time to clean a few fish to enjoy a fish sandwich or batch of finger fillets.

Pigfish are bottom-feeders. Like other grunts, they produce noise by grinding pharyngeal teeth, amplifying the noise with their air bladder.

Pigfish are caught more often in the late summer and fall. They are relatively short-lived, with a maximum life span of four years.

PINFISH
picture 79

Pinfish are rarely sought by fishermen for food or game; this lack of appreciation, however, does not prevent Pinfish from being caught frequently — they always seem to be on the hook or eating bait intended for larger fish.

Typically, Pinfish are small, measuring five to eight inches and weighing one-quarter to one-half pound; they can grow to 15 inches and two pounds. The body is oval in shape. Sharp teeth, with notched edges, line the small mouth. Pinfish are silvery in color, and a dark spot behind the gill cover is characteristic. Thin blue and yellow stripes run head to tail, and faint dark bars run top to bottom.

Like Sheepshead, Pinfish are members of the porgy family.

Pinfish are caught so often because they are a very common, wide-ranging species. One reason Pinfish are successful is their varied diet; they eat whatever is available, including crabs, shellfish, smaller fish, worms, and seaweed. Pinfish sometimes follow skates and rays in order to pick up scraps of food as the larger fish feed. Another reason Pinfish are widespread is that they tolerate a wide range of water temperature, salinity, and depth.

Because of their small size and a reputation of having bony meat, Pinfish are not often used for food. They are perfectly edible, however, and are tasty pan-fried, baked, or in chowder. Their small size simply means one must be willing to clean several fish to make a meal — only a couple Pinfish provide ample meat for a tasty fish sandwich. Also, their bony reputation is undeserved: Pinfish do not have more bones than other fish; they are easily filleted.

Pinfish can be used another way to provide a good meal; they make excellent live bait for larger game fish such as mackerel, grouper, drum, and Bluefish.

Small children delight in catching Pinfish. Pinfish put up a good fight for their size; using very light tackle adds to the excitement of Pinfish angling.

Care should be taken in handling Pinfish, as they are aptly named: Small spines on their fins stick fingers and hands just like pins or needles.

POMPANO
picture 80

The Florida Pompano is a smooth, platinum-sided fish, with a deeply-forked tail fin. It resembles other members of the jack family, of which it is a member. Most jacks are not used for food, at least in the U.S. Ironically, the Pompano is one of the most highly-prized species for eating; its flavor is excellent.

A slender, slab-like body and forked tail enable the Pompano to swim rapidly. Its fins, especially in younger fish, are yellow. Closer inspection reveals five or six spines in front of the high, soft dorsal fin. The Pompano's head is blunt, and the jaw is set low on its head. Unlike other members of the jack family, a Pompano lacks scutes (bony knobs) on its caudal peduncle (just in front of the tail).

Pompano are most often caught in the surf, though sometimes they are hooked in bays and estuaries. Mole Crabs or fresh shrimp make excellent bait for these fish. Pompano are exciting to catch: They put up a strong fight for their size and often make a dramatic leap out of the water right after they are hooked.

The name Florida Pompano was adopted because Florida is the main commercial source of this species. Specimens usually weigh one-half to one pound; the record Pompano in South Carolina is 8.5 pounds.

RED DRUM
picture 81

Surf fishermen hold the Red Drum in high esteem as a game and food fish. The Red Drum is further honored as the official state fish of North Carolina.

The shape of the Red Drum is long and slender. Body color ranges from silver-gray to reddish-bronze. The species is distinguished by a large black spot just in front of the tail fin (there can be multiple spots). The tail fin of the Drum is rounded in younger fish, squared-off in larger fish. The Red Drum has a large mouth that is set inferiorly on its head. Unlike some members of the drum family, there are no chin barbels on the underside of its mouth. Scales are large.

Red Drum taken while surf fishing usually weigh from one to forty pounds. The state record in South Carolina is 75 pounds; the record in North Carolina is 94 pounds, which is also the world record! Some of these huge fish are over 50 years old.

Red Drum run in schools during fall and spring migrations. They are bottom-feeders, eating mollusks, crustaceans, and small fish.

Smaller Drum caught in the surf are often called Puppy Drum. Other names for Red Drum include Redfish, Channel Bass, and Spottail Bass.

Although larger Drum are sometimes wormy, smaller fish are highly regarded as food. In fact, Red Drum, served as Blackened Redfish, is presently a popular menu item.

SEATROUT
picture 82

The Spotted Seatrout is a beautiful fish, graceful and unmistakably trout-like in appearance. The body shape is long and slender; the color is gray above and silvery below.

Numerous black spots highlight the seatrout's upper body, tail fin, and second dorsal fin. The spots on the second dorsal fin distinguish the Spotted Seatrout from its close relative, the Weakfish (Gray Trout). The spots also give rise to the other common name of the Seatrout, Speckled Trout.

The Seatrout's mouth is large; numerous teeth are present, including two fang-like teeth in the upper jaw. Not surprisingly, Seatrout are voracious predators, feeding on smaller fish, shrimp, and crabs.

The male Seatrout produces sounds; this vocalization is not surprising, as the Seatrout is a member of the drum family (along with Kingfish, Croaker, Spot, and Red Drum).

Seatrout generally weigh from one-half to five pounds. The state record in both North and South Carolina is near 12 pounds.

The Seatrout is highly-regarded as a food and game fish. Seatrout are caught in the open ocean, as well as in bays and estuaries where they come to spawn.

SHARKS

picture 83

Sharks are typically labeled "primitive" fish, in contrast to the more "advanced" bony fish. A case can be made, though, for labeling sharks as "special" fish instead of primitive fish.

True, sharks have been swimming in the earth's oceans for several hundred million years. But so have bony fish; sharks and bony fish evolved from common ancestors 300 to 400 million years ago.

And, yes, sharks differ from bony fish anatomically. Sharks have skeletons composed of cartilage, not bone. Sharks have no air bladder; they sink to the bottom if they stop swimming. Sharks have no bony gill cover (operculum), only gill slits. Sharks avoid drying in salt water by retaining the waste product urea in their blood.

Sharks, however, are unquestionably successful. Some sharks are the premier ocean hunters, with no enemies save man. Many sharks are at the top of food chains, typically preying on more "advanced" bony fish.

Also, compare shark reproduction with that of bony fish: Male sharks have claspers, adaptations of their pelvic fins, to perform internal fertilization. Shark mating produces small numbers of well-developed, large young. Many sharks, in fact, bear live young. Bony fish, on the other hand, reproduce by external fertilization. Millions of eggs and sperm are released into the water; huge numbers of planktonic larvae result, with only a few surviving to maturity.

Obviously, shark reproduction more closely approaches reproduction of "very advanced" humans and other mammals.

The "special" sharks possess remarkable sensory systems adapted for hunting: The lateral line of sharks is exceptionally sensitive, enabling them to detect movements of other animals at long distances. More impressively, special organs detect electrical fields. As the muscles of all animals generate small electrical impulses, sharks detect these impulses, and thus locate the animals (this system works on the same principal as an EKG machine recording electrical impulses in human heart muscle). Using this unique "sixth sense," a shark can spot hidden prey, such as a flounder or a ray buried in a sandy bottom.

Also remarkable is the fact that sharks are among the very few animals that almost never get cancer. Unlike bony fish, sharks are very resistant to strong carcinogens (cancer-causing chemicals). Research on what makes sharks so cancer-proof may someday help cure or prevent human cancer.

Sharks are also unique in having internal tissues, with the exception of blood, heavily colonized by bacteria (man and other animals normally have no bacteria in muscles and bones). The bacteria inside sharks do not cause disease; they may represent a symbiotic relationship not yet understood.

Perhaps sharks are labeled primitive because they attack man. But shark attacks are rather infrequent occurrences. Only ten shark attacks have ever been recorded in North Carolina waters. In South Carolina, about 40 attacks have been reported. More people in the U.S. die each year from reactions to bee stings or penicillin than die in 50 years from shark attacks. Females should feel even safer from shark attacks: For some reason, nine of ten shark attack victims are male!

About 50 species of sharks occur in Carolina waters (of 350 species worldwide). Sharks in Carolina waters measure (full grown) from six inches to fifty feet in length (rare sightings of Whale Sharks, the biggest fish in the world, have been reported off the Carolina coast). Several species of sharks that frequent Carolina coastal waters are known human-attackers. The best known human-eating species, the Great White Shark, is seen infrequently in Carolina waters; still, the largest Great White Shark taken in South Carolina waters measured more than 1,200 pounds and 15 feet long!

Several small sharks are seen on Carolina beaches or piers, but not by their own doing. The Atlantic Sharpnose, Spiny Dogfish, and Smooth Dogfish Sharks are often caught by fishermen; these sharks are considered a waste and are tossed on the beach or pier to die.

The Sharpnose and Dogfish Sharks are similar in appearance, typically measuring one to three feet long. Like most sharks, they are gray on top and white on the bottom. All have an asymmetric tail fin — the upper lobe is much larger. These species are carnivores, eating animals such as fish, crabs, and squid. The sharks roam from shallow brackish water to depths of several thousand feet. All three species migrate north in the spring and summer, and return south in the winter.

On close inspection, the Sharpnose and two Dogfish Shark species can be differentiated (diagram 23). The Spiny Dogfish has a spine in front of each of its two dorsal fins and lacks an anal fin. The Smooth Dogfish's second dorsal fin begins above a point in front of its anal fin. The Sharpnose Shark's second dorsal fin begins above the middle of its anal fin, and the Sharpnose's tail and dorsal fins are edged in black.

Diagram 23

Three small shark species, similar in appearance, are common along the Carolina coast. The Smooth Dogfish's second dorsal fin begins above a point in front of the anal fin. The Spiny Dogfish Shark has distinct spines in front of both dorsal fins. The Sharpnose Shark's second dorsal fin begins above the middle of the anal fin; the dorsal and tail fins are typically edged in black.

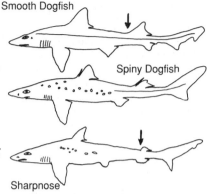

Smooth Dogfish

Spiny Dogfish

Sharpnose

Most sharks remain in the open ocean. Occasionally, a shark sighting off a Carolina beach leads to a temporary halt in swimming. Only a few sharks venture into Carolina sounds and estuaries.

The liver is a relatively large organ in sharks. Sharks do not have fat; instead, sharks store food reserves in the form of oil, most of which is in the liver. The liver oil also makes sharks more buoyant; since sharks have no air bladder, the added buoyancy is important.

Sharks are readily eaten in many parts of the world. Shark meat is beginning to gain acceptance in the U.S., but there remains a reluctance on the part of most American fishermen to utilize shark.

Part of the hesitation to eat shark stems from a lack of knowledge on proper preparation of shark meat. A shark must be bled, gutted, and iced within 20 minutes of being landed, or urea will foul the taste. Urea deteriorates into ammonia, which imparts a bitter taste to the flesh. Soaking the meat in a lemon juice or vinegar solution before cooking eliminates any remaining ammonia and whitens the flesh at the same time.

Mako, Blacktip, and Lemon Sharks, all found in Carolina waters, make excellent eating. Sharpnose and Dogfish Sharks are also quite edible.

Humans need to change their attitudes toward sharks. Instead of fear and loathing, sharks should be viewed with understanding and respect. Sharks have been swimming in the earth's oceans for hundreds of millions of years, eons before dinosaurs even appeared on earth! Sharks are a normal and useful cog in the ocean ecosystem; disrupting any part of this ecosystem could lead to unknown and undesirable consequences. Senseless "sport" fishing and overfishing for food may threaten the existence of some shark species. Several factors render sharks particularly vulnerable to man's abuse: Sharks grow slowly, reach sexual maturity late, and produce only a few young at a time.

SHEEPSHEAD
picture 84

Sheepshead are handsome fish, marked by five to seven distinct vertical black stripes on their side. The stripes give the Sheepshead its nicknames, Convict Fish and Zebra Fish. The body of the Sheepshead is whitish-silver; the head is large.

The name Sheepshead stems from prominent, broad incisor teeth in the front of the fish's mouth (the teeth resemble those of sheep). The teeth are used to chew hard-shelled animals such as barnacles, crabs, shrimp, and mollusks.

Sheepshead usually weigh from one to ten pounds; the record in North Carolina is 18 1/2 pounds, in South Carolina, 15 pounds.

Anglers like to catch Sheepshead, as they have an excellent taste. Sheepshead are a challenge to catch: They tend to nibble, instead of immediately swallowing bait. Most often, Sheepshead are caught near pilings and jetties, where they gather to chew barnacles and other food off wood and rock.

SKATES AND RAYS
pictures 86, 87, 88

Skates and rays are unusual in appearance. These fish have bodies flattened like a pancake, and pectoral fins spread from their sides into "wings" (diagram 24). Skates and rays swim by slowly flapping their fin-wings, gliding gracefully yet eerily through the water.

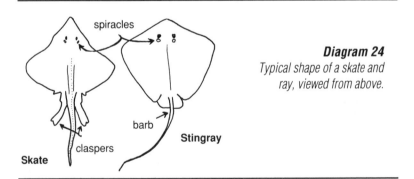

Diagram 24
Typical shape of a skate and ray, viewed from above.

Like sharks, skates and rays are classified apart from the majority (90%) of fish that have bony skeletons. Skates, rays, and sharks have skeletons composed of cartilage. Another characteristic that sets skates and rays apart from bony fish is the absence of an air bladder; skates and rays must keep moving or they will sink to the bottom.

24. Blue Crab (page 25)

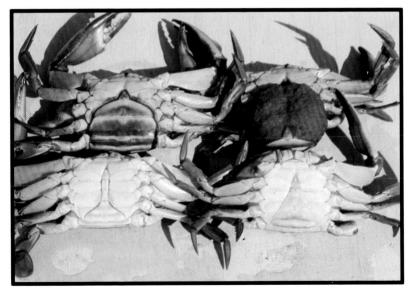

25. Blue Crabs *female, female in sponge,* (page 25)
male, immature female

26. Fiddler Crab, *male* (page 27)

27. Ghost Crab (page 28)

28. Hermit Crab (page 29)

29. Horseshoe Crab (page 30)

30. Marsh Crab (page 32)

31. Oyster Crabs (page 32)

32. Stone Crab (page 33)

33. Mole Crabs, *orange egg mass on underside* (page 35)

34. Acorn Barnacles (page 34)

35. Goose Barnacles (page 34)

36. Shrimp (page 37)

37. Spiny Lobster (page 38)

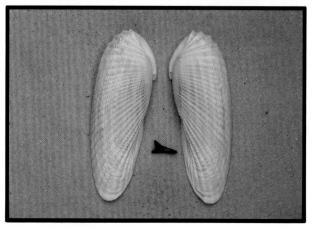

38. Angel Wings (page 43)

39. Ark Shells (page 43)

40. Auger Shells (page 44)   *Shark's tooth = one inch*

41. Clams (Quahogs) (page 44)

42. Cockle Shells (page 46)

43. Coquina Clams (page 47)

44. Cross-barred Venus Clams (page 48)

45. Disk Shells (page 49)

46. Jingle Shells (page 49)   *Shark's tooth = one inch*

47. Keyhole Limpets, *top* **, Kitten's Paw,** *bottom* (pages 50, 51)

48. Marsh Periwinkles (page 51)

49. Moon Shells (Shark Eyes) (page 52)

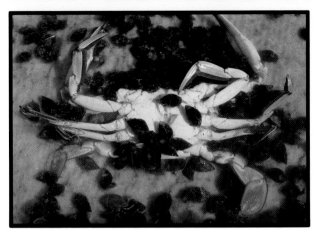

50. Mud Snails *on Blue Crab* (page 53)

51. Ribbed Mussels (page 54)

52. Olive Shells (page 55)   *Shark's tooth = one inch*

53. Oysters (page 55)

54. Oyster Drills (page 57)

55. Pen Shells, *left,* **Razor Clams,** *right* (pages 57, 58)

56. Scallops (page 59)

57. Scotch Bonnets (page 60)

58. Slipper Shells (page 61)   *Shark's tooth = one inch*

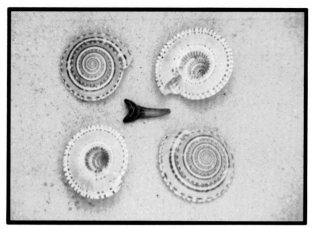

59. Sundials (page 62)

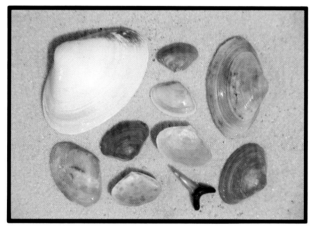

60. Surf Clams (page 62)

61. Tulip Shells, *True Tulip (left), Banded Tulip (right)*
   (page 63)

62. Turkey Wings (page 63)

63. Whelks— *Lightning (left), Knobbed (center), Channeled (right)* (page 64)

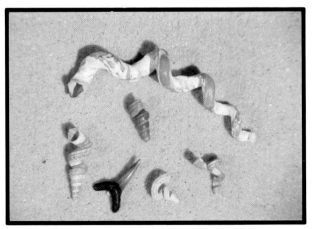

64. Worm Shells (page 65)   *Shark's tooth = one inch*

65. Bluefish (page 69)

66. Puffer (page 70)

67. Puffer, *inflated* (page 70)

68. Burrfish (page 70)

69. Croaker (page 71)

70. American Eel (page 72)

71. Flounder (page 74)

72. Kingfish (Whiting) *Northern Kingfish (top), Gulf Kingfish (bottom)* (page 75)

73. Lizard Fish (page 75)

74. Spanish Mackerel, *top,* **King Mackerel,** *bottom*
(page 76)

75. Menhaden (page 77)

76. Mullet (page 78)

77. Oyster Toadfish (page 79)

78. Pigfish (page 80)

79. Pinfish (page 80)

80. Florida Pompano (page 81)

81. Red Drum (page 82)

82. Spotted Seatrout (page 82)

83. Sharks, Atlantic Sharpnose (page 83)

84. Sheepshead (page 86)

85. Spot (page 88)

86. Cownose Ray (page 86)

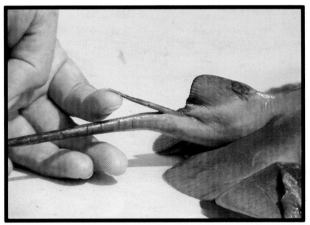

87. Stingray barb (page 86)

88. Clearnose Skate (page 86)

89. Anole (page 90)

90. Argiope Spider (page 90)

91. Coral (page 91)

92. Cannonball Jellyfish (page 92)   *Shark's tooth = one inch*

93. Portuguese Man-of-War (page 92)

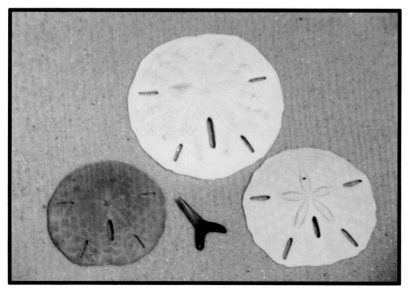

94. Sand Dollars (page 95)

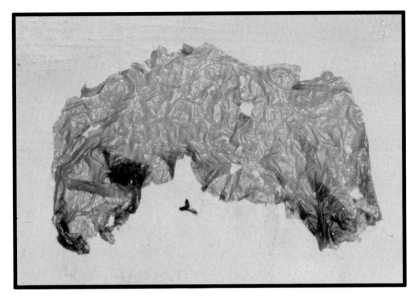

95. Sea Lettuce (page 96)

96. Sea Stars (page 97) *Shark's tooth = one inch*

97. Loggerhead Turtle (page 98)

98. Sharks' Teeth (page 101)

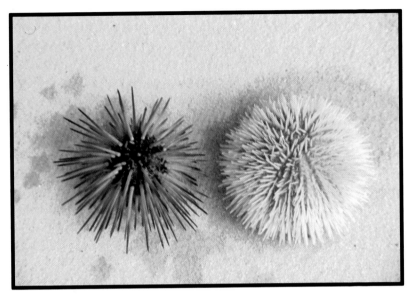

99. Sea Urchins— *Purple (left), White (right)* (page 100)

100. Sea Urchin Tests— *Purple (left), White (right),* (page 100)

101. Skate Egg Cases, *top* (page 104)
Whelk Egg Case, *bottom* (page 104)

102. Seaweed (Algae) (page 115)

103. Beach Grass (page 112)

104. Sea Oats (page 123)

Despite these "primitive" characteristics, skates and rays have been very successful; they have been swimming in the earth's oceans for hundreds of millions of years.

Skates and rays are bottom dwellers. At times, they lie still, mostly covered with sand, waiting for prey; only their eyes and spiracles (openings for breathing behind the eyes) are visible. At other times, they glide through the water, just above the bottom, stirring up mud and sand to find food.

Crabs, shellfish, worms, small fish, shrimp, and squid are eaten; skates and rays have powerful teeth and jaws for grinding up their prey. These fish can be very destructive to oyster and scallop beds.

Skates, despite an ominous appearance, are not dangerous to man. They are quite edible: Meat can be cut from skate "wings" to make an excellent meal, similar in taste to scallops. Skates are underutilized for food, however; when caught, they are often left on the beach to die.

The eggs of skates develop outside the fish's body, in the ocean. Their leathery egg cases are commonly found on Carolina beaches (see Skate Egg Case section).

The Clearnose Skate is the most common shallow-water species in the Carolinas. The distinguishing feature of this species (and reason for its name) is translucent areas on either side of the snout. Other characteristics include an angular diamond shape, long tail, pointed snout, small spines on the midline of the body and tail, and length up to three feet.

The Little Skate is found in shallow and offshore waters. The top of the Little Skate is gray-brown, with small darker spots present; the underside is white. The shape is more rounded, as is the snout. This species grows to 18 inches long.

Rays, unlike skates, can be dangerous to man; species that are harmful are termed stingrays. In contrast to skates, rays' eggs hatch and develop inside the fish's body — like mammals, they bear live young (but the young are nourished inside the fish's body by a yolk sac, not through the mother's bloodstream).

Although many sources state rays are not edible, they can be quite tasty if prepared properly. The flavor of ray meat (like shark meat) is improved if the fish is bled immediately after catching and the meat is soaked in a vinegar or lemon juice solution before cooking. These measures rid the meat of urea, which imparts a bitter taste to the flesh.

Several species of stingrays are found in Carolina waters. Stingrays possess a long thin tail characteristic of rays. The tail is armed with a venomous spine (*picture 87*). The spine is located at the base of the tail (near the body). When threatened, stingrays whip their tail back and forth, attempting to inflict a wound with the poisonous barb. Part of the barb may break off and be left in a wound.

Swimmers and waders should know how to prevent and treat stingray wounds. To keep from being stung, a wader should shuffle when walking in shallow, murky water. This will hopefully scare away a ray before the wader steps squarely on the fish, resulting in a sting.

To treat a stingray wound, the affected part should be placed immediately in hot water. Hot water inactivates protein in the poison. If the wound is more than superficial, medical attention should be sought; part of the spine may be imbedded.

SPOT

picture 85

Panfish are small fish that are easily fried in a pan. The Spot is the premier panfish in the Carolinas: This species is widespread and the taste is excellent.

Spot are small fish, usually measuring six to ten inches; they can grow to larger than a foot. Spot are silver in color, with a bluish tinge, and the fins are yellow. There is a small dark spot behind the gill cover (thus the name Spot); dark vertical stripes mark the tail end of the fish. Comparing a Spot with the similar Pinfish, the Spot is typically larger, has a blunter forehead and a lower set mouth, and lacks sharp "pins" in the fins.

Spot "runs" occur in the fall. Gill nets are used to catch tens or hundreds of fish at a time. Spot are also caught in large numbers from fishing piers and the surf. When Spot are running, piers may be lined with fishermen, each pulling in Spot after Spot.

One reason Spot occur in great numbers is that their diet is varied; Spot consume meals such as worms, crabs, shrimp, smaller fish, decayed matter, and eelgrass. Another reason Spot are successful is that they tolerate wide ranges of water temperature (35 to 95 degrees F) and salinity (fresh to full-salt of mid-ocean).

OTHERS

Included in this section are common plants, animals, and objects which do not fit into a larger category. These subjects, ranging from a spider to sea turtles to egg cases of skates, are certainly interesting enough to be included in the *Nature Guide*.

Three animals in this section can be classified together. Sea stars (starfish), sea urchins, and sand dollars are **Echinoderms**. Echinoderms are a unique group in the animal kingdom and deserve special mention.

One distinguishing attribute of Echinoderms is a water vascular system. The water system is a network of canals and reservoirs running throughout the animal's body, typically branching into tube feet on the animal's outer surface. Tiny suction cups are present on the ends of the tube feet.

Through manipulation of their tube feet, Echinoderms grasp objects in their environment; in this manner, Echinoderms use the water system as other animals use muscles — for movement, food transfer, and holding onto objects.

Another feature of Echinoderms is a radially symmetric body design consisting of five equal parts. In other words, Echinoderms exhibit a design like a pie divided into five equal pieces.

Echinoderms possess an internal skeleton of calcium carbonate. The skeleton is not an external shell, as might be thought at first glance. While the skeleton may be close to the animal's surface, a layer of living tissue always covers the skeletal plates; even the spines of sea urchins and sand dollars are covered by a thin layer of skin.

Bumps and spines on the outer surface also characterize Echinoderms. The name Echinoderm stems from Greek words meaning "hedgehog skin."

Echinoderms are exclusively marine: There are no fresh-water or land-based members of this group.

89

ANOLE
picture 89

The Anole is a small, bright green lizard, common to the Carolinas. It is also known as the Green Anole or American Chameleon.

Anoles are often seen lying in a sunny place, motionless. Like other reptiles (lizards, snakes, turtles), they are cold-blooded, so their body temperature nears that of their environment. They bask in the sun to warm their bodies, enabling their metabolism to function at a higher rate.

throatfan of male

When Anoles do move, they run very swiftly on their four legs. They are able to roam horizontal or vertical surfaces (trees, sides of houses) with ease. This ability to move up and down even vertical surfaces helps them to capture prey (insects) and avoid predators.

Anoles have another interesting method of escaping predators. If a predator (or human) grabs an Anole's tail, the distal tail breaks off, allowing the Anole to escape (the predator is left "holding the tail"). The Anole, like other lizards, is able to regenerate its tail.

Contrary to popular belief, Anoles do not change color in order to match their background and camouflage themselves from predators. Anoles change color in response to temperature, light, or confrontations with other members of their species. They can transform from brown to bright green within minutes. The ability to change color accounts for Anoles being sold as chameleons at circuses or as American Chameleons at pet stores. Technically, though, Anoles do not belong to the true chameleon family whose species reside in Africa.

Male Anoles have an expandable red throatfan. Males exhibit the bright throatfan in territorial and defensive displays.

Anoles can grow to nine inches long. They have five small claws on each foot and prominent toe pads that help them hold tightly to surfaces.

Anoles are quite harmless, and they make good terrarium pets. Anoles must be fed live insects, however; crickets are a favorite meal.

ARGIOPE SPIDER
picture 90

The Argiope Spider is striking in appearance, both in color and size. Bright yellow and white spots highlight the Argiope's jet-black body. With its long, spindly legs, the spider measures several inches wide.

The Argiope, like other spiders, has eight legs and a body divided into two sections: a cephalothorax (head/chest) bearing the legs and an abdomen bearing several pairs of spinnerets (web spinners). Spiders are not insects but arachnids; other arachnids, closely related to spiders, include ticks, scorpions, and mites.

The Argiope feeds on insects, such as mosquitoes and flies, snared in its web.

The web of the Argiope is almost as impressive as the spider itself. An Argiope's web is an intricate circular pattern, three to four feet in diameter! The size and pattern of the web make it easily visible from a distance. The web is most often located in the upper marsh, but yards and gardens adjacent to marshes also provide habitat for the Argiope.

CORAL
picture 91

Coral washed upon the beach has the look and feel of a stone indented with tiny, round, flower-like pits. It is easy to see coral for what it is, the supporting structure of a whole colony of coral animals — sort of a calcium carbonate condominium.

An individual coral polyp lives in each two- to three-millimeter pit. The polyp's body is a small tube; a mouth surrounded by tentacles is located on one end (diagram 25), and the other end is permanently attached in its home. The polyp is sessile (unable to move about its environment). The body and tentacles are extended from the pit to trap food.

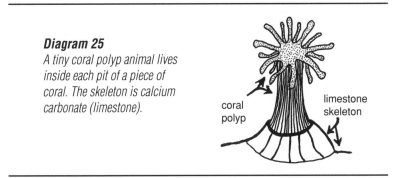

Diagram 25
A tiny coral polyp animal lives inside each pit of a piece of coral. The skeleton is calcium carbonate (limestone).

coral polyp

limestone skeleton

Like jellyfish, coral polyps possess nematocysts; these stinging cells paralyze the very small creatures the polyps feed on.

Each coral polyp secretes its own pit and foundation made of calcium carbonate. The calcium carbonate of adjacent polyps meets, forming the skeleton of the colony. After the polyps die, only the hard skeleton is left.

The skeletons of different coral species vary widely in size and shape. Rod and blob shapes are common.

Coral grows mainly in tropical waters; coral reefs are found only in warm seas. It is not uncommon, though, to find a piece of coral on Carolina beaches. There are two reasons coral appears here: 1) Two types of coral grow in cooler Carolina waters. 2) Even corals normally found in tropical waters may grow in our area.

Star Coral is one type that grows in colder water; it survives as far north as the Arctic Ocean. Colonies of Star Coral look like a flat, non-branching blob growing on a rock or shell (diagram 26). The color is white to brown. Five to thirty animals usually make up a colony; a colony can reach five inches in diameter.

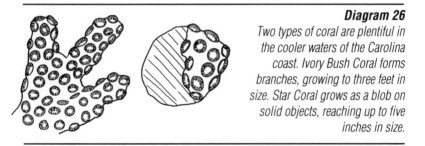

Diagram 26

Two types of coral are plentiful in the cooler waters of the Carolina coast. Ivory Bush Coral forms branches, growing to three feet in size. Star Coral grows as a blob on solid objects, reaching up to five inches in size.

The other coral growing in cooler water is Ivory Bush Coral. Bush Coral colonies form branches and can reach three feet in size. When alive, the colony is red-brown; after dying, the colony bleaches white.

Tropical corals (as well as tropical fish) appear in small numbers as far north as Cape Hatteras. The presence of tropical species is due to the offshore Gulf Stream, which brings warm waters of the Caribbean north; the warm water brings tropical species along with it.

Corals produce larvae that are microscopic zooplankton. These free-floating forms are spread far and wide by ocean currents. Most perish, either eaten by predators or coming to rest on bottoms unsuitable for growth. Those that land on a hard substrate are able to begin new colonies.

JELLYFISH
pictures 92, 93

Jellyfish are not true fish; rather, they are primitive, floating marine animals. Jellyfish are invertebrates (no backbone or spinal cord); they are the simplest creatures integrating individual cells into muscle fibers and a nervous system.

Two sections typically make up a jellyfish: 1) a round jelly-like body providing swimming or flotation, and 2) long, thin tentacles for trapping prey. Generally, jellyfish are transparent or translucent (see-through). The tentacles of some species can inflict painful stings on swimmers and waders.

Most jellyfish can swim by a pulsing action of their jelly dome, but large-scale movement on the ocean's surface is dictated by currents, tides, and winds. Jellyfish are pelagic, meaning they inhabit the open ocean far from land. At times, usually in the summer, large numbers of jellyfish appear nearer shore. Jellyfish may even wash up on the beach, where they die.

Jellyfish seen by beachgoers are actually one of two alternating stages in the life cycle of these animals. The mature medusa stage is the typical globular-tentacled form seen on the beach or in shallow waters. The medusa moves about, reproduces sexually, and dies at the end of a single season. The other, infrequently seen stage is the polyp form; a flower-like polyp is much smaller, tubular, attached to one place, and reproduces by asexual budding (producing planktonic young).

The Cannonball Jellyfish, also known as the Cabbage Head or Jellybomb, is the most common species seen in Carolina waters and shores. The Cannonball's jelly body is a firm, milky-white ball, with a brownish band around its edge; up to eight inches in diameter, the body is translucent, so orange-red internal organs are clearly visible. The lower part of the Cannonball is a stalk with short arms. The Cannonball Jellyfish lacks true tentacles. Most sources indicate the animal does not sting humans, though some individuals have reported mild stings from contact with Cannonballs.

The Portuguese Man-of-War is also found in Carolina waters. Though the Man-of-War resembles a jellyfish (diagram 27), it is technically classified as a siphonophore (siphon bearer).

The Man-of-War is mainly a warm-water species, but specimens are transported northward by the Gulf Stream; easterly winds then blow Man-of-Wars near shore.

Diagram 27
The Portuguese Man-of-War has a gas-filled, translucent blue float; tentacles trail up to 60 feet in the water.

A Man-of-War's float is translucent blue, pear-shaped, and filled with gas like a balloon. The tentacles are long, dragging up to 60 feet or more behind the animal. Interestingly, the Man-of-War is not a single animal, but a colony of hundreds of attached organisms, mutually dependent on one another.

Each tentacle on a Man-of-War has about 750,000 nematocysts on it. A nematocyst is a tiny capsule containing toxin and a coiled thread-like barb. Upon contact, the barb shoots out, lodging in prey or enemies. The toxin stuns the Man-of-War's prey (small fish and other animals). Each nematocyst, like a bee stinger, can be used only once; nematocysts are continually replaced.

When a human comes into contact with a Man-of-War, nematocysts fire automatically, inflicting multiple stings. A linear, welt-like wound results, which is very painful. Very rarely, deaths occur, probably due to severe anaphylactic (allergic) reactions to the stings.

Stings can be avoided by watching for Man-of-Wars when swimming. If present, Man-of-Wars should be given wide berth to avoid the long tentacles. Man-of-Wars should not be touched even when washed up on the beach, as the nematocysts can still inflict stings.

Studies have shown that <u>vinegar</u> is an excellent solution to apply on stings to neutralize the toxin. Strong pain medicine may also be required to control the discomfort. Anyone with breathing difficulties or generalized body swelling is showing signs of a severe allergic reaction: They should be taken immediately to the closest emergency facility for aggressive treatment.

Jellyfish, as well as Man-of-Wars, are eaten by giant Ocean Sunfish as well as by sea turtles. The Sunfish and turtles are apparently not affected by nematocysts.

In some parts of the world, jellyfish are eaten in the form of a paste or dried flour. None are typically eaten in the Carolinas.

PLANKTON

Plankton are immensely important microscopic plants and animals that make all other sea life possible. They literally form the base of oceanic food chains.

These tiny plants and animals are among the most abundant forms of life on earth; in one drop of sea water there may be hundreds of plankton.

PHYTOPLANKTON (plant plankton) are actually the main producers in the ocean; their essential function consists of making living material (food) out of inorganic matter (basic elements and non-plant/animal life). This process, using energy from the sun, is called photosynthesis. The vast pastures of the oceans contain an estimated 80 percent of the earth's vegetation in the form of phytoplankton!

Phytoplankton exist in an infinite variety of shapes and sizes (diagram 28). They are moved about at the mercy of ocean currents (phyto=plant, plankton=wanderer).

Diagram 28
Microscopic plankton grow in a vast array of science fiction shapes.

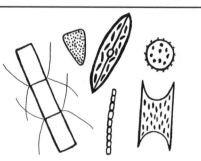

ZOOPLANKTON (animal plankton) are also swept from place to place by ocean currents (zoo=animal, plankton=wanderer). Some zooplankton are permanent members of the plankton community, as they remain small in size and are always moved by the water. Other zooplankton, though, are only temporary members of the zooplankton zoo. Most temporary forms are larvae of larger animals; they eventually develop into big, free-moving animals. Among animals that begin as zooplankton are barnacles, crabs, mollusks, and Horseshoe Crabs.

How do plankton form the basis of oceanic food chains and all ocean life? Phytoplankton make living matter from inorganic material. Zooplankton feed upon phytoplankton and other zooplankton. In turn, larger animals feed upon both types of plankton; plankton consumers include bivalves (clams/scallops/oysters), barnacles, jellyfish, some fish (menhaden, manta rays), gastropods (snail-like animals), and even baleen whales.

In turn, animals that feed directly on plankton are eaten by other, larger animals. This is what is meant by a "food chain": progressively larger animals feeding on smaller prey. Consider a few simple oceanic food chains: Phytoplankton are eaten by shrimp-like krill, which are eaten by baleen whales. Plankton are eaten by menhaden, which are eaten by blue-fish, which are eaten by man. In this way, plankton form the very basis of ocean life.

Plankton can also cause problems for man. Phytoplankton, being dependent upon sunlight, tend to reproduce and grow more rapidly in warmer weather. At times, a plankton bloom occurs, with tremendous numbers of one type of plankton reproducing.

A dramatic plankton overgrowth causes "red tide," where hundreds of millions of one type of organism (a unicellular dinoflagellate) are found in a cubic meter of sea water. The red tide kills other algae, fish, and shellfish in its vicinity; alga particles also become airborne, causing irritation to human respiratory passages. Red tide is a misnomer, as the red coloration is slight when visible and often not seen at all.

Most plankton are found in the upper layers of ocean waters, where sunlight provides energy for photosynthesis. Coastal waters have much more plankton than the open ocean; drainage from land yields nutrients necessary for abundant plankton growth.

SAND DOLLAR

picture 94

Sand dollars are shaped like cookies: round, flat, and thin. Like their close relatives, starfish and sea urchins, sand dollars exhibit a five-part radial symmetry (like a round pie cut into five pieces).

The five-part pattern is obvious in the Keyhole Urchin, the most common sand dollar found on Carolina beaches. Keyhole Urchins usually measure three to five inches in size, and possess five keyhole-shaped openings in the body. On both the top and bottom of the shell is a five-petaled, flower-like design.

While alive, sand dollars are covered with a layer of brown-to-green, fine, velvety spines. The animals use their short spines to slowly plow through the top layer of loose sand. When sand dollars wash up on the beach and die, they quickly lose this coating. The shell, or skeleton of the animal, bleached white by the sun, is what beachcombers find.

As a sand dollar "walks," tubes with suction discs on the ends, called tube feet, move food to the central mouth. The small organic particles and animals so gathered are chewed by the dentary apparatus in the mouth. It is the remnant of this dentary apparatus (sometimes called Aristotle's Lantern) that rattles when a sand dollar skeleton is shaken.

Sand dollars live on the ocean bottom. They gather in beds lying parallel to the shore.

To reproduce, adult sand dollars release sperm and eggs directly into the water. If fertilization occurs, planktonic larvae result; the larvae are bilaterally symmetric (with two equal sides on either side of a line dividing the animal). After passing stages as free-floating plankton, the animals metamorphose into radially symmetric adult-shaped animals, settling to the bottom to live.

Many fish eat sand dollars, including flounder and cod. Sea stars (starfish) also prey on sand dollars. Humans, of course, gather sand dollars from beaches and shallow waters, but not to eat. Instead, sand dollars are used for jewelry and decorations — as they have been used throughout man's history.

SEA LETTUCE

picture 95

Although actually an alga, Sea Lettuce washed up on the beach looks like a piece of wilted, bright-green garden lettuce. Its edges are ruffled and somewhat irregular. To the touch, Sea Lettuce has the feel of waxed paper. A sheet of sea lettuce is tough, even though it is very thin (actually only two cells thick).

Sea Lettuce grows in shallow water, attached by a holdfast to shells, rocks, and plants on the bottom. It frequently breaks off in rough surf and either remains as a free-floating plant or washes up on the shore.

Sea Lettuce is an important source of food for many marine animals and waterfowl.

Though widely used in the Orient for human food, Sea Lettuce is not commonly eaten in the U.S. Although tough, it is easily chopped up for use in salads; Sea Lettuce can also be cooked in soups.

Sea Lettuce can be harvested from shallow water, especially during the spring and early summer. After picking, it should be thoroughly washed in fresh water. Small holes in the fronds mean tiny snail-like animals have grazed on it, but the Sea Lettuce is still perfectly safe and good to eat.

In some places, Sea Lettuce is so abundant that it is used for hog food. Unusually dense concentrations, however, can indicate overgrowth due to the release of excessive nutrients and pollutants into the water.

Like other algal plants, Sea Lettuce has no true roots, stems, leaves, or flowers. Sea Lettuce reproduces by producing floating spores instead of seeds.

SEA STARS (STARFISH)
picture 96

Sea stars (starfish) are characterized by their five-armed star shape. As these creatures are not true finned fish, scientists prefer the name sea star to starfish.

Sea stars are closely related to sand dollars and sea urchins; like them, they exhibit radial symmetry and move about by tube feet.

Upon closer inspection, sea stars range in color from light orange to red to purple, or even greenish-black. The mouth is on the underside, in the center. Four rows of tube feet line the underside of each arm; a tiny red eye sits at the end of each arm. Openings of sex ducts occur at each arm junction. The size of a sea star depends on the amount of food it has consumed, not its age.

Sea stars are sometimes carried long distances by ocean currents. Normally, though, movement is accomplished with tube feet, appendages like distensible pipes with suction cups on the ends. Water is taken in through skin pores, then pumped into the tubes, lengthening the tube feet. By coordinating which feet are expanding and which are contracting, sea stars advance one arm at a time, moving a few inches a minute.

The tube feet of sea stars are also used for feeding. Starfish are carnivorous, preying on mollusks such as oysters, clams, cockles, scallops and mussels.

When a sea star locates a clam, it settles on it, placing three arms on one side, two on the other. Using its tube feet to grasp the shell firmly, it attempts to pry the clam open just a crack. If successful in opening the clam even a fraction of an inch, a sea star everts its stomach out its mouth and into the clam shell. The sea star then digests the soft parts of the clam, draws its stomach back in, and moves on. Using this method, a starfish can eat up to six or eight clams a day.

Naturally, sea stars are disliked by shellfishermen. Before much was known about sea stars, shellfishermen may have unwittingly increased sea star populations. When caught in fishing nets, sea stars were cut or broken into pieces, then thrown back into the sea. The fishermen didn't know that a starfish is able to grow new arms, a process called regeneration. In some sea star species, one arm can regenerate a whole animal!

The ability to cast off injured arms, and to regenerate new arms, accounts for sea stars being found with fewer than or more than five arms.

Sea stars sometimes wash up on the beach, where they die. Live specimens can be found underneath rocks at low tide. While sea stars usually inhabit shallow water, they have been found to depths of several thousand feet. Sea stars are absent from upper estuaries, as they can survive only in water greater than 16 to 18 parts per thousand of salt.

To reproduce, sea stars shed sexual gametes directly into the water. The tiny larvae join the zooplankton community; after many changes they metamorphose into recognizable sea stars about one millimeter in size. Within one year, sea stars grow to a breeding size of about 2.5 inches.

Brittle stars are a group of animals related to sea stars. Brittle stars are distinguished by a distinct central disc and long, snaky arms (diagram 29). They move faster than sea stars; the sinuous movements of their arms give them the nickname "serpent stars." Brittle stars are also more fragile than sea stars; their arms break off easily when handled.

Diagram 29
Brittle stars are similar to sea stars. Brittle stars are distinguished by a distinct central disc and long, snaky arms.

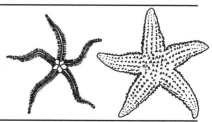

SEA TURTLES
picture 97

Sea turtles are reptiles; that is, they are cold-blooded, air-breathing, scaly-skinned vertebrates (backboned).

Like all turtles, sea turtles possess a toothless beak and a soft body encased in a hard shell. Unlike land or fresh water turtles, sea turtles have legs modified into flippers (even the webbed feet of fresh water turtles end in distinct toes).

Only seven species of sea turtles exist in the world today — all are in danger of extinction.

Five of the seven species are found in waters off the Carolina coast, including the Loggerhead, Green, Hawksbill, Atlantic (Kemp's) Ridley, and Leatherback. Only the Loggerhead is commonly seen here, and it is the only species to nest regularly on Carolina beaches. Rare nests of Green, Leatherback, and Ridley turtles have been reported in the Carolinas.

Loggerhead Turtles live in open ocean and estuarine waters. The female, however, makes brief returns to the beach in the summer to lay eggs. At night, she crawls out of the ocean, up the beach to just above the high tide line.

The nesting Loggerhead most often locates her nest at the seaward base of the primary dune line. She scrapes out a depression in the sand with her flippers. Up to 150 round, leathery, golf ball-sized eggs are deposited in the pit. The female Loggerhead covers the eggs with sand and then crawls back into the ocean. The whole egg-laying process takes about one hour.

Loggerheads lay their eggs late at night, so they are not frequently observed on the beach. Turtle tracks are more likely to be seen the day after a turtle lays eggs. Two rows of tracks (coming and going) are present between the ocean and egg-laying site; the tracks resemble the marks a small bulldozer would make in sand.

Female Loggerheads usually nest every other year or every third year. One to seven (two or three typically) clutches of eggs are deposited during a nesting season.

Loggerhead eggs incubate 45 to 80 days. After hatching, the baby Loggerheads crawl upward from the nest but remain just below the beach surface for one to three days. The hatchlings, just a few inches long, emerge at night as a group. As they scurry down the beach into the ocean, the turtles are susceptible to predators such as Ghost Crabs, raccoons, and gulls.

Male turtle hatchlings never return to the beach; their life is a mystery. Female hatchlings return an estimated 13 to 30 years hence to lay eggs. Females probably return to the same beach where they hatched.

Interestingly, Loggerheads are temperature-sex-dependent (TSD). Sea turtles have no X or Y chromosome to determine sex. Instead, the sex ratio of a Loggerhead nest is determined by the temperature of the sand surrounding the nest during incubation. Under laboratory conditions, as incubation temperatures are raised above 84.5(F) degrees, progressively more females are produced. As temperatures are lowered below 84.5(F), progressively more male hatchlings result.

Loggerhead Turtles grow to more than three feet in length and weigh 200 to 500 pounds. Although large, Loggerheads can paddle through water at speeds up to 25 mph. An active sea turtle surfaces to breathe every five to fifteen minutes. However, when a turtle sleeps, its body metabolism slows down; far less oxygen is required. In a sleep state, a sea turtle can remain under water for up to three hours!

Juvenile and adult sea turtles are preyed upon by sharks, grouper, and Orcas. Loggerheads, in turn, feed on jellyfish, mollusks, fish, shrimp, squid, and Horseshoe Crabs. Loggerheads even eat the Portuguese Man-of-War, which can inflict painful stings on man.

Loggerheads sometimes ingest plastic bags, mistaking the floating trash for a jellyfish. The bags can lodge in the digestive tract of a turtle, preventing normal movement of food; the turtle may die of starvation. The danger trash poses to Loggerheads is another reason humans must learn not to throw trash into the sea.

It is a sad commentary on our civilization that these magnificent and benign turtle species are endangered or threatened. The decrease in turtle populations is clearly man's doing. Direct predation on turtles for meat, eggs, and shells has reduced their numbers. Thousands of sea turtles drown annually in the nets of shrimp and fish trawlers. Development of coastal beaches has destroyed turtle nesting habitats. Baby turtles and turtle nests are run over by all-terrain vehicles. And, finally, artificial lighting near nesting beaches disorients baby turtles, causing them to head landward instead of seaward.

Sea turtle populations are declining. Loggerheads have been classified as threatened (not endangered) since 1978; as such, they remain protected by law (Endangered Species Act) and should not be disturbed on the beach.

Some individuals believe that the loss of sea turtles and other species is the inevitable result of progress. This concept of progress is short-sighted; we know little about long-term consequences to life on earth with the continuing extinction of species. Each species of plant or animal has its own niche in nature; when a species is removed, the effect on the whole ecosystem may be profound, and man may suffer in the end.

SEA URCHIN

pictures 99, 100

A live sea urchin resembles a pincushion: The urchin has a round center covered by a mass of thin spines. An appropriate nickname for the urchin is the "sea porcupine."

The movable spines of a sea urchin extend from a hard shell, or skeleton. The spines fall off when the urchin dies. Usually, only the shell is found by a beachcomber, and the shell is often bleached white by the sun before being found.

Looking closely at a sea urchin shell, rows of varying-sized bumps are seen, running from the top to bottom of the shell. Rows of tiny, pinpoint holes are visible between the bumps. The urchin's spines attach to the shell at the bumps; the sea urchin's tube feet protrude through the holes.

Two species of urchins are common to the Carolinas. The Purple Sea Urchin varies in color, ranging from purplish to dark red to even brown or black. The shell of the Purple Urchin grows to two inches wide by three-quarter inches high. Although this species is most often found in shallow water, it does live in depths up to 200 feet.

The other species of urchin common to the Carolinas is the White Sea Urchin. The White Urchin has shorter spines and lives at greater depths than the Purple Urchin.

Sea urchins live in protected locations: in rocky areas and tidal pools, near jetties and pilings, and among seaweed. There, they hide in cracks and crevices, gaining protection from predators and currents. Urchins are typically found in beds (groups) of various-sized urchins, not as lone animals.

A sea urchin, like its sand dollar and sea star (starfish) relatives, has a body divided into five equal radial areas. The urchin's mouth is on its underside, the anus on top. The mouth consists of five tooth-like plates, used for scraping food off solid objects; the mouth is very similar to a sand dollar's mouth and is similarly called "Aristotle's Lantern." With this chewing apparatus, the urchin eats algae and small invertebrates and scavenges on dead animals as well.

Also like its sand dollar and sea star relatives, the sea urchin possesses hundreds of tube feet. An urchin uses its tube feet to attach firmly to hard surfaces.

An urchin's tube feet are located all over its body between its spines. A water pump system is used to vary the size and length of tube feet. Water is brought into the urchin through microscopic pores on its upper surface, then channeled into tube feet on one part of the animal. The feet in that area are lengthened, the suction discs on the feet ends grasp an object, and the rest of the animal is pulled along. Using this system, an urchin is able to move in any direction, at a speed of one to two inches a minute.

Many animals prey on sea urchins, including sea stars, conchs, oyster-catchers, gulls, crabs, and many fish.

Humans, too, use sea urchins for food. Urchin eggs are considered a delicacy in the Orient; in the U.S., they are rarely eaten.

Both the White and Purple Sea Urchin produce delicious roe. Preparing urchin eggs is time-consuming but easy; the eggs are simply scraped from the inside of a cleaned shell. Like caviar, urchin eggs are eaten raw.

Urchins are often used by scuba divers to attract fish. If a diver crushes an urchin with a rock or knife, small fish gather quickly to eat the innards of the urchin. Divers must handle an urchin with care, though, as sharp urchin spines can easily penetrate skin.

SHARKS' TEETH
picture 98

Occasionally, a beachcomber scanning the sandy beach is lucky enough to find what is obviously a tooth; the tooth is dark in color, and one-half to several inches in length. The lucky find is a shark's tooth; the size, shape, and color of the tooth vary with the species of shark (each tooth can be identified as to which species of shark it came from).

The teeth of about 14 shark species are found on Carolina beaches; among those found are teeth of Great White, Hammerhead, Tiger, Bull and

Lemon Sharks. Several of these species are known to attack man. Imagine what a mouth full of hundreds of these teeth could do to any animal!

Rest assured, though — the teeth found beachcombing are not from sharks currently alive. They are fossil teeth, from sharks living thousands to millions of years ago. Dark teeth found on the beach are all fossils. A tooth from a modern-day shark is white and is rarely found on the beach.

Shark teeth are, in fact, about the only remnant from ancient sharks. Unlike most fish, with skeletons composed of hard bone, sharks have skeletons composed of softer cartilage. But, like man, the hardest substance in sharks' bodies are their teeth. Thus, when sharks die, their bodies decompose, except for their teeth, which can survive for eons.

Sharks produce a large number of teeth during their lifespan, which is another reason some teeth survive to surface on today's beaches. It is estimated that a Tiger Shark, for example, produces up to 24,000 teeth in a ten-year period! Sharks not only have rows of functioning teeth in place, they also maintain 5 to 15 rows of backup teeth. Sharks do not have to wait until they grow new teeth to replace lost ones: As functional front teeth are lost, reserve teeth move forward to replace them.

SHIPWORM

Beachgoers often find pieces of wood, riddled with holes and tube-like burrows, washed up on the beach. The cause of damage to the wood is not apparent at first glance. Did termites on land chew the wood before it became water-borne? Or could there be marine termites that ravaged the wood?

Marine animals called Shipworms, in fact, make the worm-like burrows in wood exposed to the ocean. Interestingly, Shipworms are not really worms, but worm-like bivalve mollusks (clam-like animals), complete with small shells. They are specially adapted to burrow in wood.

Most of the adult Shipworm's body is soft and worm-like (diagram 30), reaching up to one foot in length. On one end of the body are two vestigial shells, one-half inch in size. The bivalve Shipworm uses the shells to scrape wood, lengthening its burrow; the surface of the shells has fine ridges and teeth to scrape away tiny pieces of wood.

Diagram 30
The body of a Shipworm is worm-like. Shipworms are not true worms, but mollusks, as they have two vestigial shells on one end of the body.

shells

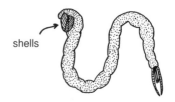

On the other end of the Shipworm's body are two siphons. The incurrent siphon brings in water from which the animal extracts oxygen. The excurrent siphon removes waste products.

The larvae of Shipworms begin life as microscopic zooplankton. After several weeks free-floating in the ocean, the larvae must find wood to settle on in order to survive. Larvae lucky enough to find wood metamorphose to adult form and begin digging a tiny hole in the wood.

A Shipworm spends the rest of its life in the same piece of wood. As the Shipworm grows, it excavates and lengthens its burrow. The burrow is lined by a layer of calcium carbonate secreted by the Shipworm's mantle. The width of a Shipworm burrow is about one-quarter inch (6 mm); wood riddled with burrows of this size is diagnostic of Shipworm infestation.

Shipworm-infested wood

Shipworms damage wood more than is obvious to the eye. The entrance hole to the burrow, visible from the surface, is small (the Shipworm never enlarges the entrance hole). However, the burrow winds deep into the wood. Wooden structures infested with Shipworms may suddenly fall apart from the damage.

As Shipworms bore, they follow the grain of wood; they turn aside to avoid a knot in the wood or another Shipworm's burrow. A Shipworm removed from its burrow is unable to excavate another one.

By boring into wood, Shipworms receive two benefits. First, the tunnel protects the soft worm-like animal, much like a shell protects other mollusks. Second, Shipworms use wood as food. Wood is composed of hard-to-digest cellulose; Shipworms maintain populations of bacteria in their gut that produce enzymes to digest cellulose.

In addition to riddling driftwood, Shipworms damage ships, pilings, and docks. Destruction to man-made structures costs millions of dollars annually. The nickname of the Shipworm, "Termite of the Sea," is appropriate. Creosoted and "treated" lumber is resistant to Shipworm penetration.

All Shipworms begin life as males. Some remain male, while others change to female later in life. Males shed sperm directly into the water. Fertilization occurs if sperm is drawn in through a female Shipworm's incurrent siphon.

Shipworms are worldwide in distribution. They are able to survive from the Arctic to the Tropics. At least six species are found in Carolina waters.

SKATE EGG CASE

picture 101

The egg case of the skate is a black leathery object, three to four inches long; it is rectangular in shape, with a curly horn at each corner. Nothing else like it is found on the seashore. Who would guess that this curious object comes from the skate, a flat fish that swims by fluttering along just above the bottom? (see skates in the fish section).

When a female skate lays an egg case, it is attached to underwater plants with a sticky substance and a structure called a holdfast. The egg case is also held in place by a pair of curly tendrils, which extend from one end of the egg case, near one pair of horns.

The horns on the corners of the egg case serve to extract oxygen and release waste into the water.

Each egg case is formed around a single egg with a large yolk. As an embryonic skate grows inside the egg case, it is protected from predators. The young skate hatches as a miniature adult, ready to fend for itself (no larval stages for this animal). The empty egg case later loosens from its mooring and washes up on the beach.

Because of their purselike shape, skate egg cases are also called "devils' pocketbooks," "mermaids' purses," or "sailors' purses." Perhaps the last name is the most appropriate, as the egg cases almost always wash up empty!

WHELK EGG CASE

picture 101

A pretty shell is not the only object a whelk leaves for beachcombers to enjoy; the egg case of the whelk is also frequently found on ocean beaches.

The whelk egg case is a spiraling strand of parchment-like hollow discs, connected to a string like a necklace. The egg case is as light as paper. At first glance, the individual discs appear to be round and the size of a penny but, upon closer inspection, they are actually irregular ovals.

Each individual disc initially contains up to a hundred or more eggs. Many of the eggs never hatch, as they are eaten by newly-hatched siblings. Tiny whelk hatchlings, about the size of a pinhead, first hatch inside the disc; they later "hatch" a second time as they eat their way out of the disc. Each animal emerges as a tiny miniature whelk, just like its parents in form.

A tiny hole is usually visible in each disc, where the young whelks have escaped. Rarely, the capsules wash up intact with the eggs or hatchlings still inside.

The capsules from different species of whelks vary in shape. The capsule edges of the Knobbed Whelk are flat and square, whereas the capsule edges of the Channeled Whelk are sharp.

WHALES AND DOLPHINS (CETACEANS)

Whales and dolphins are not fish but aquatic mammals. Like humans and other land mammals, they breathe air with lungs, are warm-blooded, have hair at some time in their lives, bear live young, and nurse their young on milk.

Whales are divided into two groups: toothed whales and baleen whales.

Toothed whales, which are smaller and more common, have peg-like teeth. The teeth enable the whales to prey on fish, squid, and other large marine animals. Sperm Whales, Orcas, and dolphins are all toothed whales (dolphins are actually small, toothed whales). Toothed whales have just one blowhole on the top of their head.

Baleen whales are larger and less common than toothed whales. Baleen whales have no teeth in their mouth; instead, fringed sheets of baleen hang down from their upper jaw. To feed, baleen whales open their jaws, filling their mouth and throat with water. The water is then

Baleen (Right) Whale   **Toothed (Sperm) Whale**

forced out, straining it through the baleen. Plankton, small crustaceans, and tiny fish are trapped on the baleen. The whale wipes the baleen with its tongue and swallows the tiny animals whole.

Baleen whales have two blowholes on the top of their head. Blue Whales, Humpback Whales, and Right Whales are baleen whales.

Amazingly, whales and dolphins evolved from land mammals, which had evolved from sea animals eons ago! The paddle-shaped anterior flippers of whales and dolphins evolved from mammalian forelegs (they have no hind flippers or external hind limb remnants). The blowholes on top of their heads correspond to the nostrils of land mammals. Thus, cetaceans, as whales and dolphins are collectively known, returned to the oceans and found their own niches.

One might think that breathing air would limit cetaceans' swimming ability in the ocean. But some whales dive up to 1,000 feet, staying under water 40 minutes! Several adaptations enable whales to breathe more efficiently: Their muscles have a large amount of myoglobin, which stores oxygen. Also, a whale exhales much more of the air in its respiratory passages with each breath than other animals; up to 90% of oxygen-depleted air is exhaled and replaced with fresh air during each spouting (a man replaces about 10% of the air in his respiratory passages with a normal breath).

Cetaceans are intelligent animals, possessing relatively large brains. They communicate with each other by voice; noises are made by forcing air through nasal passages. Whales and dolphins are social animals, often traveling in groups. Like humans, they bear live young one at a time, and they exhibit caring behavior while raising their young.

Whales and dolphins can detect objects in their surroundings using a sonar-like system; they send out sound waves and locate objects by returning echoes. The system is so precise that a blindfolded dolphin can easily pinpoint and retrieve objects in the water.

More than 70 species of cetaceans travel the oceans; of these, 50 are dolphin species.

Dolphins are regularly seen in Carolina waters, both in the sounds and off the beach. Usually, dolphins are sighted as they travel in a small group; the animals periodically surface to breathe as they swim.

The sighting of a dolphin dorsal fin is sometimes mistaken for a shark fin, causing unnecessary fear. Observation of a fin reveals whether it belongs to a shark or dolphin. A shark, with a vertical tail fin, will have a dorsal fin and tail fin visible as it swims. A dolphin, with a horizontal tail fin, does not exhibit a tail fin (until it breaches the water to dive). Also, a dolphin swims with an undulating motion (up and down), while a shark swims with a zigzag motion (side to side).

Rumors have circulated that the presence of dolphins in the water means that no sharks are nearby, as the two types of animals are natural enemies. On the contrary, both groups of animals feed on the same schools of small fish, sometimes in the same location.

Dolphins are also called porpoises. Even scientists argue about which traits make a dolphin and which a porpoise. To complicate matters, there is a type of fish called a dolphin. Unless a person is an expert on dolphins, the terms dolphin and porpoise can be used interchangeably to designate these fish-like mammals.

Whales other than dolphins are seen much less often in Carolina waters. Occasionally, large whales are sighted swimming miles off the coast. These whales are migrating back and forth from cold water areas (where they live) to warm water areas (where they breed and give birth). Interestingly, whales do not feed while migrating.

Rarely, a whale beaches itself, creating much excitement. Often, the whale is still alive when it comes ashore. Unfortunately, the sheer weight of the whale acts to crush its internal organs; compression of the lungs slowly suffocates the animal, and efforts to rescue the whale are most often fruitless.

The exact reason a whale beaches itself remains a mystery. Experts speculate that parasites affect the echo-location organ of the whale, causing it to lose navigational ability. For now, the definite reason for whale-beaching remains unknown.

The magnificence of whales is epitomized in one astonishing fact: Whales are the largest animals <u>ever</u> to inhabit the earth! The Blue Whale, four times heavier than any dinosaur that roamed the earth, can grow to more than 100 feet and 300,000 pounds. Whales are able to sustain an enormous body mass partly because water supports their great weight.

Sadly, the Blue and many other species of whales are near extinction. The U.S. no longer permits whaling, but countries such as Japan, Norway, and Iceland still maintain whaling fleets.

When you're at the beach, you're in the mountains, too.

(Sand is particles of quartz
eroded from inland mountains.)

COASTAL ENVIRONMENT

Both North and South Carolina are blessed with a varied and attractive coastal environment. Habitats include ocean, sandy beaches, sand dunes, maritime forests, salt marshes, tidal flats, bays, estuaries, and sounds.

The Carolina coast is a far cry from the New England seacoast. The Northeast coast is rocky and meets the sea with a steep, abrupt border.

The junction of land and sea in the Carolinas is dominated by sand or mud — beach and marsh predominate. Very few rocky areas exist on the Carolina coast; a few natural outcrops of coquina rock and man-made rock jetties are the exceptions.

The broad, flat Carolina coastal plain converges with the ocean very gradually. Marshland, which is part terrestrial, part aquatic, is the result of this gentle blending of land and sea.

The Carolina coastal environment is fairly uniform overall. As a result, the common marine animals of this region belong to the Carolina Faunal Province.

The Carolina Faunal Province actually encompasses a larger area, from Cape Hatteras to Cape Canaveral, Florida. The animals of the Carolina Province form a fairly distinct group, separate from the units to the north (Virginian Province) and south (Caribbean Province).

Most would agree that the Carolina coast is beautiful, serene, and peaceful. Yet the beauty of sandy beaches and picturesque marshland should not obscure the importance and fragility of the coastal environment. The true beauty of the coast is more than sand deep.

Each component of the coastal environment, from beach to sound, plays an essential part in the overall beauty. Each habitat is separate and beautiful in its own right, yet intricately intertwined into the whole — no part stands alone. The deeper beauty of the coast resides in its overall environment. In other words, the whole is greater than the sum of its parts.

The importance and inter-relatedness of each coastal habitat means that the richness of the environment as a whole is susceptible to damage from deterioration of even one component. If marshes are filled, fish and crabs that grow up there will disappear from the ocean. If dunes are levelled to build high-rises, beaches in front of the dunes will eventually be lost.

The fragile coast is threatened NOW. The threat is from mankind. Prompt commitments are necessary to protect our priceless coast. Men and women need to care enough to take action.

The following sections highlight components that make up the wonderful potpourri of the Carolina coast.

BARRIER ISLANDS

The concept of barrier islands is essential in understanding the Carolina seacoast.

Barrier islands are islands and peninsulas which parallel most of North and South Carolina's coasts. The islands can be likened to parts of a necklace embracing the body of the mainland (diagram 31). Barrier islands are separated from the mainland by bodies of water that vary in size, from narrow segments of the intracoastal waterway to huge bays and sounds.

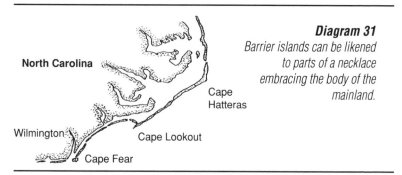

North Carolina

Cape
Hatteras

Wilmington

Cape Lookout

Cape Fear

Diagram 31
*Barrier islands can be likened
to parts of a necklace
embracing the body of the
mainland.*

South Carolina (35) is second only to Florida (80) in the number of barrier islands on its coast, and North Carolina is not far behind (23).

From oceanside to backside, a barrier island can be divided into separate zones: ocean beach, primary dunes, secondary dunes, maritime forest, salt-water marsh, and tidal flats (diagram 32). Maritime forest is present only on wider islands.

Barrier islands are fully exposed to the ocean. They experience the brunt of normal winds, tides, and waves as well as the full fury of sporadic coastal storms and hurricanes. As such, they serve as a buffer between the ocean and the mainland, and thus the name "barrier."

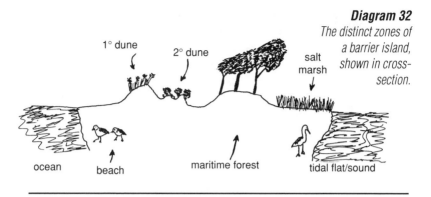

Diagram 32
The distinct zones of a barrier island, shown in cross-section.

These everyday and storm forces of nature keep barrier islands in a constant state of flux: The islands erode in one area, build up in another. Barrier islands continually absorb the blows and fury of nature, then bounce back. This cycle of damage and repair is thousands of years old. Net damage is nil — when the islands are left in a natural state.

Man's development of barrier islands interrupts and alters the natural cycle of damage and repair. It is only on developed islands that millions of dollars in damage result from a storm. Damage on a developed barrier island is especially large when the fragile and changing <u>oceanfront</u> is built upon.

When nature's forces act on developed barrier island oceanfronts, erosion threatens man's structures. The erosion is hastened if development has removed the protective dunes (which is often the case). Buildings can literally fall into the sea.

Historically, as man's structures are threatened, artificial structures are constructed in an attempt to halt erosion; such structures include seawalls, jetties, and groins. These structures do protect man's buildings for a while — but, they also result in the loss of the beach.* Ironically, the artificial structures actually accelerate beach erosion, and the beach is swallowed up by the sea. All that remains are the buildings, seawall, and sea — there is no beach to walk on.

The loss of beach is a tragedy because the beach belongs to the public: Public beach is lost to protect private property!

Some states are learning (slowly) from past mistakes and are taking measures to prevent the loss of public beach in this manner. Examples of ways in which public beach can be protected include: 1) Instituting set-backs for oceanfront construction, and 2) outlawing artificial seawalls and jetties. North Carolina, in general, has been more protective of its beaches than South Carolina.

Beach renourishment, or the artificial replacement of sand on beaches, is another solution to coastal erosion. Sand replenishment is temporary; the new sand erodes, too, and the beach must be renourished often if erosion is significant. Renourishment is also expensive, and the cost is borne by all taxpayers, not just those who live at the beach.

The best solution to barrier island development is to strictly limit development, especially anywhere near the oceanfront or inlets (inlets are also prone to erosion).

Population density is another problem that needs to be addressed concerning barrier island development. The density (number of residents per square mile) on Carolina barrier islands is more than four times the national average. High population density places great stress on the fragile barrier island environment. Overpopulation ultimately results in pollution and destruction of the very things that attracted people to these areas: Water is polluted, marshes are destroyed, shellfish beds are contaminated, and so on.

Sometimes one wonders if building on barrier islands should be permitted at all. Once one sees an undeveloped barrier island, the thought arises: Wouldn't it be nice if barrier islands were preserved unchanged, for all the public to enjoy? Perhaps access roads and parking facilities should be the only man-made structures allowed on barrier islands!

The installation of artificial structures with resultant loss of natural beach is known as "New Jerseyization" of the seacoast. Many New Jersey beaches have been lost to the cycle of development, rapid erosion, construction of seawalls, and loss of beach.

BEACH GRASS
picture 103

American Beach Grass, like Sea Oats, is one of the very important plants that build and maintain the foredunes of the beach. Though not native south of Cape Hatteras, Beach Grass has been planted extensively to stabilize dunes in the Carolinas; it grows quite well on our coast.

Beach Grass grows on sand dunes as separate clumps of green grass, reaching a height of three feet. The long, thin, green leaves of Beach Grass are not accompanied by stalks of seed plumes (in contrast to Sea Oats).

When Beach Grass is planted on a dune, grains of sand collect around the plant as sand is blown over the surface of the beach. The sand that gathers at the base of the plants actually stimulates further plant growth. The cycle of sand collection and plant growth continues, stabilizing the sand dune in the vicinity of the grass.

Beach Grass spreads by rhizomes (root-stems) that run a few inches under the sand. New plants grow out of nodes on the rhizomes. In this manner, other areas of the foredune are stabilized.

American Beach Grass has adapted to survive the harsh foredune environment. Water is scarce, temperatures vary widely, and salt spray is carried landward on ocean breezes. Beach Grass has an extensive root system to capture water. In dry, hot weather, the leaves of Beach Grass curl about its stem, like corn husks around an ear of corn; the curling serves to slow evaporation of water through the plant's pores.

Ridges on each blade enable the leaf to curl. Ten to twelve ridges run the length of the grass blade on its upper surface. These ridges, easily seen with the aid of a hand lens, also identify the plant as Beach Grass.

Another name for American Beach Grass is Compass Grass. This nickname arises from compass-like circles the wind-bent leaves scratch in the sand.

HURRICANES

If nothing else, remember two things about hurricanes: 1) IF A HURRI-CANE APPROACHES, GET AWAY FROM THE COAST, and 2) GET AWAY EARLY, LONG BEFORE THE STORM STRIKES!

Hurricanes are large, violent tropical storms, with winds of 75 mph or greater. The winds rotate in a circular, counterclockwise (north of the equator) motion around a center of low pressure.

The winds, while a force to be reckoned with, are not the major threat from a hurricane. Rather, the main danger stems from **storm surge** caused by the winds. Storm surge is the rise in ocean sea level above normal; it may reach 15 to 25 feet above normal water level. The storm surge, along with accompanying storm waves, batters the coast with awesome force. Most of this tremendous pounding is absorbed by the first 100 yards landward from the ocean. Thus, oceanfront buildings and structures suffer the most damage in a hurricane (although soundside flooding can be extensive and damaging as well).

Likewise, the major threat to human life is storm surge, not the wind. Ninety percent of lives lost in a hurricane typically result from storm surge and rising water levels.

Interestingly, storm surge is also responsible for the formation of inlets. Sound waters back up to very high levels during a hurricane. Once the hurricane passes, the pent-up water surges back to the ocean. As a result, inlets (maybe they should be called outlets) are formed where the water takes the easiest route through a barrier island to the ocean.

Thus, storm surge is the major hurricane force to be reckoned with, causing economic loss, deaths, and inlet formation. Damage from winds, though, is no minor problem. Winds may reach 190 mph, as with Hurricane Camille in 1969. Also, tornadoes can spin off hurricanes, causing severe localized damage.

Does it seem that hurricanes have gotten worse in recent years? The damage from each successive hurricane mounts into more millions, that's for sure. Hurricanes haven't changed, though. What has changed is the amount of coastal development. As more and more construction takes place, damage from a hurricane (and potential fatalities) rises. There is no doubt that major hurricanes will continue to strike our coast, catching coastal residents and visitors off guard, with resultant staggering losses of property and lives.

Hurricane season runs from June 1 through November 30. August, September, and October are the months of highest hurricane incidence. The greatest potential for loss of human life occurs in August, since oceanside resorts are full, making evacuation more difficult.

The average number of hurricanes forming per year is six; the most ever forming in a year was twelve. North Carolina is at higher risk of hurricanes hitting its coast than South Carolina or Virginia: North Carolina extends outward into "hurricane alley" and is exposed to the path of more storms.

On the average, a hurricane strikes the North Carolina coast about every three years. The variation is tremendous, though, as a hurricane may not strike the North Carolina coast for 20 to 30 years, but three or more hurricanes may strike the coast in one year.

Until 1989, the Carolinas had been lucky: Over the prior100 years, the top ten hurricanes in terms of deaths, intensity, and cost of damage struck elsewhere in the United States. Hurricane Hazel, striking the Carolinas in 1954, ranked in only the top twenty in these destructive indices.

Hurricane Hugo, in 1989, struck a devastating blow to the Carolinas. Hugo was the 10th strongest hurricane to strike the U.S. mainland to this time. In terms of deaths, Hurricane Hugo fortunately didn't even make the top twenty. However, in dollar damage, Hugo was the costliest hurricane ever to hit the U.S. mainland. Hurricane Andrew, ravaging Florida in 1992, supplanted Hugo as the costliest hurricane. Hurricanes Fran (1996) and Floyd (1999) targeted the Carolinas and joined Hugo in the "top ten" hurricanes in terms of fiscal loss. Future storms will surely surpass even these titans of destruction as coastal development continues.

The National Hurricane Center in Miami, Florida, tracks hurricanes, issuing statements about the danger and need for evacuation from each storm. A Hurricane Watch is issued when a hurricane poses a threat to land and is 24 to 36 hours from the coast. A Hurricane Warning is issued if the threat is between 12 and 24 hours from land.

Heed the warnings issued by the Hurricane Center! Again, the best piece of advice concerning hurricanes is: GET OUT, AND GET OUT EARLY! Hurricanes should always be taken seriously. Don't be impressed by media stories about people who "rode out the storm." It is ignorant to stay on the coast to protect property; there is little one can do when the storm hits, and one's very life is at risk. Remember, too, that a hurricane floods roads long before hitting land, so early evacuation is wise.

MARINE PLANTS / SEAWEED / ALGAE
picture 102

The vast majority of marine plants are algae. Algae are simple plants: They do not possess true roots, stems, leaves, or flowers (though they can have similar-looking structures). The need for specialized plant structures is obviated, as algal plants are able to absorb nutrients, carbon dioxide, and water over their entire surface.

Microscopic, free-floating algae are known as phytoplankton. These small but extremely important algal plants are discussed in the section on plankton. Suffice it to say, phytoplankton are the cornerstone of all life on earth.

Algae also proliferate in the form of much larger, multicellular, easily visible marine plants. Though many people think of algae as simply greenish slime covering rocky surfaces, algal plants go far beyond this; algae exist in a myriad of shapes, sizes, and colors.

Almost every "seaweed" found washed up on the beach is, in fact, an alga. Many are leafy in shape, such as Sea Lettuce. Tree-branch, filamentous, and other forms are also seen. Sizes range from just above microscopic to ten-foot kelp (120-foot giant kelp on the West Coast is also an alga). The color of algal plants ranges from green to blue-green, red, and brown; the colors emanate from different light-capturing pigments, which vary with the intensity of light where the algae grow.

Most larger algae grow on the bottom, in shallow water close to shore. There, they anchor by structures called holdfasts to shells, rocks, or other solid matter. Holdfasts are not roots, as they are not specialized for absorbing nutrients. Storms and rough seas sometimes pull the holdfasts loose and wash the plants on shore.

Some species of seaweed/algae are free-floating, remaining at the surface where they obtain maximum sunlight for photosynthesis. Sargassum seaweed, of which there are many species, is typical of the floaters. Pea-sized air bladders are interspersed among its fronds, keeping the plant afloat.

Grass species are also important marine plants. Grasses, unlike algal plants, are true flowering plants, with roots, stems, leaves, and flowers. Eelgrass is the predominant grass species off the Carolina coast. The blades of grass serve as sites of attachment and shelter for numerous marine plants and animals. Beds of eelgrass thus serve as important nurseries for many species.

MARITIME FOREST

Maritime means "near the sea." Maritime forest groves are located close to the ocean. Tracts of maritime forest are generally located on the back (sound) side of barrier islands.

Because of its proximity to the sea, maritime forest is a unique habitat. Several factors render maritime forest unlike any other forest: Trees and bushes in maritime forest must tolerate the sandy soil of barrier islands. More significantly, the plants must survive salt spray and strong winds blown inland off the ocean.

The key species in maritime forests are trees that have adapted to the windy, salt-spray environment. These salt-tolerant plants not only survive, they also form a leafy, protective canopy. Underneath the canopy, salt-sensitive species, otherwise doomed to perish, are able to grow.

Maritime forests develop <u>behind</u> primary and secondary dunes of barrier islands. On dunes closest to the ocean, only grasses and a few bushes can endure. Trees are unable to gain a foothold — even the hardy, salt-resistant trees of the maritime forest succumb to the heavy salt spray.

Behind the frontal dunes, maritime forest begins. Even there, the effects of salt spray are noticeable: The trees closest to the ocean absorb the brunt of wind and salt spray, stunting their growth. The trees assume a characteristic wedge shape, slanting away from the ocean (diagram 33).

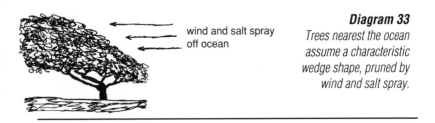

wind and salt spray
off ocean

Diagram 33
Trees nearest the ocean assume a characteristic wedge shape, pruned by wind and salt spray.

Salt-tolerant trees and bushes of the maritime forest include Live Oak, Laurel Oak, Loblolly Pine, Slash Pine, Sable Palmetto, Wax Myrtle, Red Cedar, and Yaupon Holly. Salt-sensitive species include many types found elsewhere: maples, dogwoods, persimmons and magnolias. The salt-sensitive species survive only because the umbrella of salt-tolerant species protects them.

The salt-tolerant and salt-resistant species generally vary with climate: Species show a gradual change from the cooler coast of upper North Carolina to the semi-tropical coast of lower South Carolina. The Live Oak is an exception to this generalization: As a rule, Live Oaks are associated with and dominate maritime forests from Cape Hatteras to Hilton Head.

Indeed, Live Oaks have come to symbolize maritime forest.

Live Oaks are large, squat trees — a short, thick trunk is topped by a wide dome of branches and leaves. Live Oaks are evergreen trees, not in the common sense of the word (pine trees with needles), but in the true sense of the word (remaining green through the winter). Live Oak leaves are shed every spring, but the process is gradual, and the trees are never without greenery.

Live Oak leaves are two to five inches long and elliptical in shape. A waxy coating protects the leaves from salt spray and the hot sun. Flowers appear on Live Oaks each spring; acorns fall from the trees in autumn.

Live Oaks and maritime forests have played an important role in man's East Coast history. Indians hunted game such as deer, turkeys, and squirrels under the forest canopy. Indians also ate the same Live Oak acorns that attracted game to the maritime forest.

In colonial times, Yaupon Holly leaves were used for tea. Yaupon leaves were even shipped north to supply American colonists defying the British tea tax.

Later, in the years between the Revolutionary and Civil Wars, Live Oaks came into great demand for shipbuilding. The wood in Live Oaks is very dense, the hardest wood found in any oak tree. Although too hard for cabinets and furniture, Live Oak wood proved ideal for hulls and frames of wooden ships. As a result, extensive areas of maritime forest were scourged for large Live Oaks. Some areas of maritime forest have yet to recover from the pillaging; other areas received a reprieve with the advent of steel ships.

Today, maritime forests face a new threat — coastal development. Tracts of ever-scarcer maritime forest are being replaced by condominiums, vacation homes, motels, shopping centers, and roads. Most remaining maritime forests are privately owned, likely dooming them to replacement with man-made structures.

The continuing destruction of maritime forests is ill-advised and unfortunate: The value of maritime forests goes far beyond their aesthetic beauty. Maritime forests provide a refuge for wildlife, including deer, raccoons, foxes, and birds. More importantly (at least to man), precious ground water is retained by maritime forests; dunes are stabilized by maritime growth. And, maritime forests cool barrier islands by absorbing the sun's heat.

The loss of remaining maritime forests would be a tragedy. Public attention is beginning to focus on the plight of this unique timberland habitat. Carolina lawmakers must take measures to save some of our valuable, historical maritime forests.

MARSH

Marshes, like swamps, are wetlands. In marshes, grasses predominate; in swamps, bushes and trees are the main flora. Salt water marshes, then, are wet, grassy areas; they can occur any place land and sea meet. As a rule, salt marsh grasses are exposed and dry at low tide, and at least partially water-covered at high tide.

An unthinking, outdated concept regards marshes as worthless land, suitable only for draining and filling, then developing. Nothing could be further from the truth!

Marshes are not only places of beauty — they are also areas of great economic importance. Marshes are some of the most productive land on earth. Using photosynthesis, marsh grasses convert vast amounts of solar energy into plant tissue; as the grasses die, large nutrient loads are released into adjacent estuarine waters. The estuarine system cycles nutrients to support food chains that produce the majority (scientists estimate up to 95 percent) of commercially valuable fish and shellfish in our sounds and oceans. Many of these species literally grow up in marsh-estuarine ecosystems.

Examples of fish which are OSEND, or Ocean-Spawned, Estuarine-Nursery Dependent, include croaker, drum, flounder, kingfish, menhaden, mullet, and spot. These species spend the early parts of their lives in marsh estuary areas, finding plentiful food to feed on as well as protective habitat to escape predators.

Thus, the importance of marshes goes far beyond their boundaries. For economic reasons alone, marshes need respect and protection.

Interestingly, although plants abound in marshes, relatively few plant species are present. A small number of spartina grass species, in fact, dominate marshes. Common names of this group include cordgrass, saltmarsh cordgrass, marsh grass, marram, and spartina.

Spartina grass species adapt to the harsh marshland conditions: alternating wetting and drying with tides, salinity varying with rainfall and tide levels, high winds, constant waves, and a limited oxygen supply in the marsh mud. One way spartina grass compensates for salinity is by excreting salt crystals to conserve water.

Marsh sediments are stabilized by spartina much as sand dunes are stabilized by Sea Oats and Beach Grass. Spartina grows taller near the water's edge, smaller near higher land. When spartina grass dies, the decomposed matter provides a major source of food for estuarine inhabitants.

Certain animals also tolerate rugged marsh conditions. Marsh periwinkles, mussels, and fiddler crabs thrive in this environment.

A marsh often smells rather pungent at low tide; this smell is normal.

Marsh muck (slimy black mud) is an oxygen-poor environment. Anaerobic (not using oxygen) bacteria in the muck emit hydrogen sulfide, producing a "rotten egg" odor.

OCEAN

The ocean — quite simply, is what makes our coast; its force shapes the coastal environment, attracting visitors and residents alike. But what is this huge ocean off the Carolina coast?

The Atlantic is the name given to our ocean. Along with the Pacific, Indian, and Arctic Oceans, it comprises the four major ocean basins. Man's separation of oceans is artificial, though: The world ocean is actually one interconnected system, constantly mixed by winds, tides, and currents. The continents can be thought of as islands in this single vast ocean.

The world ocean, of which our Atlantic is a part, covers roughly 70 percent of the earth's surface, at an average depth of greater than two miles. This amount of water sounds enormous, but compared to the mass of the earth, the water mass is small. If the earth were the size of a 12-inch desk globe, the ocean would be only a thin film of water on its surface.

The oceans contain 98 percent of the water on earth. This salty pool of ocean water is intimately connected with the other pools of water (so essential to life), freshwater and groundwater. A constant recycling occurs between the pools: Sunlight evaporates fresh water from salty oceans, clouds form, and rain is released over land, replenishing fresh and groundwater stores, which flow once again into the seas (diagram 34).

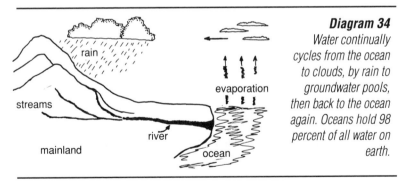

Diagram 34
Water continually cycles from the ocean to clouds, by rain to groundwater pools, then back to the ocean again. Oceans hold 98 percent of all water on earth.

The Atlantic portion of the vast uni-ocean is very fertile, supporting a dense and varied growth of plants and animals. Two types of currents serve to maintain the Atlantic's productivity: 1) upwelling currents, and 2) the Gulf Stream.

Upwelling currents bring water from the deep ocean floor to the surface.

Along with the water come nutrients in the form of decayed organisms from ages past. The nutrients, along with sunlight, provide for a rich growth of plankton. Plankton, of course, supports the oceanic food chains.

The bountiful plankton growth results in the somewhat murky, blue-green-brown color of the oceans off our coast. The murky hues thus represent a healthy, teeming ocean.

Contrast the Carolina ocean with tropical waters. Tropical waters, clear, pristine and blue, should be teeming with life. In the Tropics, though, despite a plethora of sunlight, a relative lack of nutrients exists. Without nutrients, a much smaller total production of plankton and other life occurs.

The Gulf Stream, which comes within 20 miles of the Carolina coast, is a second major influence on the variety of life in the Carolina Atlantic. Flowing northward from the coast of Florida, the Gulf Stream brings warm water with it — in volume, 25 times that of all earth's rivers put together! Not only does it bring warm water to the Carolinas, the Gulf Stream also brings warmer weather and sweeps along many species of tropical plants and animals that would not otherwise be found so far north.

Interestingly, the Gulf Stream is not like a river, with a beginning and end. Rather, it is an enormous wheel-like current traveling in a clockwise direction, winding past the coasts of Europe and Africa before returning (diagram 35). Perhaps a better name for the Gulf Stream would be the Atlantic Circular Current.

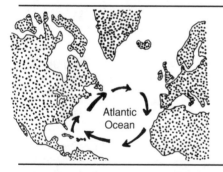

Diagram 35
The Gulf Stream is a circular current, not like a river with a beginning and end.

The Gulf Stream is, in fact, one of several large circular ocean currents traveling clockwise in the Northern Hemisphere and counterclockwise in the Southern Hemisphere.

SAND

Sand is what makes our beaches...but what is it, really? By definition, sand consists of small particles from .06 to 2 millimeters in size (a pinpoint to pencil lead). Sand particles in the Carolinas are mostly quartz, a component of most rocks of the world. Small and varying amounts of shell particles, organic wastes, and assorted minerals also form Carolina sand. Shell particles, of course, arrive on the beach as millions of generations of mollusk shells are broken down.

But where do the Carolina sand quartz particles come from? Very likely, they come from rocks and mountains on land as they erode due to wind and rain. With erosion, small pieces of quartz and feldspar, the main components of rock, are washed into rivers. The feldspar degenerates into fine particles, which are deposited in estuaries and carried offshore. The quartz is worn down into grains, which are deposited at the mouths of rivers. From there, offshore currents carry the quartz grains up and down the coast, depositing them on the shoreline and forming beaches. Thus, the beaches of the Carolinas originate from rocks in the interior highlands of the Carolinas!

Standing on a sandy beach, one might guess that the beach is relatively void of life. On the contrary, the spaces and moisture between the grains of sand are teeming with life. This life is not visible to the unaided eye; it consists of single-celled plants and animals and other microscopic organisms (diagram 36). It is hard to imagine the extent and activity of this tiny world we see only with a microscope.

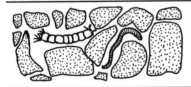

Diagram 36
Microscopic plants and animals thrive in spaces between sand grains on beaches.

So, the next time you lie on the beach, remember three things: First, you are lying on another world, one teeming with microscopic plants and animals. Second, the soft sand you are relaxing on is actually a bed of quartz rock! Third, when you're at the beach, you're in the mountains, too.

SAND DUNES

Sand dunes are the picturesque mounds of sand just behind ocean beaches. The first row of dunes adjacent to the ocean are primary dunes or frontal dunes. Dunes behind these are known as secondary dunes. Not only are dunes aesthetically pleasing — more importantly, they protect everything landward of them. Dunes protect barrier islands from wind, waves, and storms, much as the barrier islands protect the mainland from these forces.

Dunes are formed through the interaction of three key elements: sand, wind, and plants.

Sand, of course, is supplied by the beach. Wind at the shore is nearly constant, whipping the sand about. Plants of the dune stop the sand as it is blown; the sand accumulates at the base of the plants, building the dunes.

The essential dune plants must be very hardy to survive the desert-like conditions of the beach. They must endure several elements: salt spray carried by the wind, temperature extremes, constant winds, small nutrient and water content of sand, ocean flooding during storms, and intense sunlight.

Plants that are able to survive in a salty environment are called halophytes; they adapt to either absorb extra water or rid themselves of excess salt.

Very few plants survive the harsh conditions on primary dunes; Sea Oats and Beach Grass are the most successful. More species (but still not many) can survive on secondary dunes.

The importance of dunes, and the plants that stabilize them, is simple: Dunes protect everything behind them; they absorb pounding of waves, lashing of wind, and the brutal energy of storms. Not only do dunes protect man-made structures, they also protect maritime forests and the valuable marshes.

What are the threats to dunes (and to what they protect)? Mother Nature, for one: Everyday erosion, Nor'easter storms, and the infrequent hurricane all take their toll. But — dunes are able to shift and change with the impact of wind, waves, and storms, as they have for thousands of years.

The biggest threat to dunes is, in fact, man. Oceanfront construction too often involves knocking down the protective dunes. ATVs (all-terrain vehicles), too, take a tremendous toll on the dunes. These go-anywhere vehicles run over and destroy dune plants. Without plants to stabilize the mounds of sand, the dunes are more easily eroded by wind and waves.

When the dunes are destroyed, sand is washed back into the marshes, destroying them. Without marshes, our "nurseries of the sea," the animals of the sounds and oceans suffer.

One wonders: Do people destroying dunes, be it for pleasure or profit, by ATV or bulldozer, not realize they are destroying the beauty that attracts us all to the seashore? Or, do they just not care?

SEA OATS

picture 104

Consider the harsh conditions ocean dune plants endure: constant salt spray, strong winds whipping particles of sand, burning heat, numbing cold, sandy soil, salt-water flooding during storms, and burial beneath shifting sands. It's a wonder plants survive at all on the dunes!

Actually, very few plant species can live on primary dunes (the first row of dunes, right next to the ocean). Plants that are found there have adapted to the harsh conditions and dominate the area.

Two grasses, especially, dominate the primary dune zone: Sea Oats and Beach Grass. Sea Oats, ranging from Virginia to Texas, are the dominant natural dune plant in the Carolinas. Beach Grass is the dominant introduced dune plant along our coast.

Sea Oats not only survive on the dunes — they are essential stabilizers and builders of dunes as well. The roots of Sea Oats hold sand in place; the grass leaves stop and collect blowing sand. Without Sea Oats, dunes would soon be decimated by storm flooding and wind.

The main part of the Sea Oats plant is long-stemmed grass; in addition, Sea Oats display separate, distinctive stalks up to six feet tall, capped by seed pods. In the spring, Sea Oats and Beach Grass are hard to tell apart; both are green grass. Later, Sea Oats grow the picturesque stalks, topped by seed plumes. The plumes remain through early winter. In mid-winter, the stalks and leaves of Sea Oats turn brown and die back to the ground. Beach Grass, in contrast, remains partially green, even in winter.

Shifting sand on the dunes may partially or totally bury Sea Oats. Sea Oats not only survive burial — burial actually stimulates the plants to grow faster.

Like Beach Grass, Sea Oats are salt resistant, and the leaves of grass curl in hot weather to conserve moisture.

Sea Oats expand their dune coverage in several ways. New plants rise from root structures called rhizomes and from seeds off adult plants. Storms sometimes fragment plants, spreading pieces over the dunes as well.

The name Sea Oats comes from the appearance of the seeds, which resemble common oats. Very few seeds survive to grow into adult plants. Just a few of the twenty or more seeds on each spikelet are viable. The viable seeds have a chance to grow only if they are quickly buried, as birds and rodents eat the fallen seeds.

The picturesque beauty of Sea Oats contrasts with the actual hardiness of these plants. The contribution of the sixth S of the beachscape (sea/surf/sand/sun/sky/sea oats) is significant.

SEA WATER

Sea water in oceans and sounds comprises 98 percent of the water on earth. Sea water is composed of a solution of water, salts, and small concentrations of virtually all other natural elements.

The salt found in sea water is mostly NaCl (table salt), along with small amounts of other salts. Sea water is remarkably consistent in salt content and chemical compostion among the oceans of the world.

The salinity of sea water is expressed in percent salt, or parts per thousand of salt to water: If the concentration of sea water is 30/1,000, think of it in terms of 30 cups of salt dissolved in 1,000 cups of water (or 3 cups salt per 100 cups of water, equal to 3 percent salt).

Variation in salinity occurs when fresh water from land mixes into seawater. In the middle of the Atlantic ocean, the concentration of salt is 36/1,000; the concentration just off the Atlantic coast is near 30/1,000. In estuaries, where rivers meet the sea, and in sounds behind barrier islands, salinity varies: Concentrations run from 5/1,000 in upper estuaries, to between 15/1,000 and 25/1,000 in most sound areas.

The human body is 0.9 percent salt, or 9/1000; thus, our body is one-quarter as salty as mid-ocean water. This difference in salt concentration means humans can't drink salt water: Instead of supplying needed water, salt water actually draws free water out of the body.

Most animal species are unable to tolerate large changes in salinity and are thus restricted in habitat. Oysters, Blue Crabs, and American Eels are exceptions, as they tolerate a wide range of salinity as well as lower salinities.

The salinity of sea water accounts for the fact that sea water freezes less readily than fresh water. As salinity increases, the freezing point decreases. The salt in sea water also accounts for its better buoyancy (people float better) compared with fresh water.

TIDAL FLAT (MUD FLAT)

Tidal flats are broad, flat, muddy expanses adjacent to marsh. Typically, tidal flats are located on the backside of barrier islands or at the outflow of mainland tidal creeks. In contrast to bordering marsh, tidal flats appear open, barren, and still.

Tidal flow is the dominating force on tidal flats. Twice a day, water flows in and out, alternately submerging and exposing the flat. At high tide, the mud is covered with several feet of water; at low tide, the substrate is exposed to air. The salinity of water covering tidal flats varies with rain, tide, heat, and humidity.

The mud of tidal flats gives them the nickname mud flats. The thick muck substrate is actually a mixture of mud and sand. Tiny silt and clay particles are mixed with small sand grains. In addition, organic debris from decay of nearby marsh mixes with the silt and sand to form a fine, blackish mud.

Tidal flat mud also receives nutrients from the twice-daily tidal flow: Microscopic plankton and decaying matter float in with tidal water, settling on the bottom.

The combined nutrients from marsh decay and tidal flow mean tidal flats might support a rich growth of fauna and flora. At first glance, tidal flats appear rather void of life. Upon closer inspection, though, tidal flats prove to support a plethora of wildlife.

Mud Snails are the most obvious creatures of tidal flats. The half-inch black snails pepper the marsh mud. Sea Lettuce is also present in abundance, at least in the spring and summer.

Naturally, microscopic algae and zooplankton abound in the water/mud/sunlight/bountiful nutrient environment of tidal flats.

Numerous animals that filter-feed on the plankton also reside in tidal flats. Oysters, living on the mud surface, are the most visible of the filter feeders.

Numerous other filter feeders are not so obvious or visible. These animals burrow and hide from sight in the muddy substrate. Burrowing animals include clams, other bivalves, worms, and shrimp-like animals. These animals burrow for several reasons: 1) to prevent drying out at low tide, 2) to escape extremes of hot and cold (open flats may freeze or sunscald to 140 (F) degrees), and 3) to escape predators.

Some predators live on tidal flats, remaining through the tidal cycle. Such animals include Moon Snails, Knobbed Whelks, Oyster Drills, and Hermit Crabs.

Other predatory animals only visit tidal flats at specific cycles of the tide. Fish and crabs move freely into the flats at high tide, retreating to deeper water at low tide. Willets, egrets, herons, ibises, and raccoons, on the other hand, seek prey at periods of low tide.

The ample wildlife of tidal flats is largely supported by the first inch of muddy bottom sediment. Oxygen penetrates only about the first inch of muck; here, a rapid and abundant growth of algae and other plankton occurs.

Below an inch, tidal mud is relatively void of oxygen. Burrowing animals live there, maintaining tubes to obtain oxygen from the surface. Other life is limited to anaerobic (living without oxygen) bacteria.

Anaerobic organisms produce hydrogen sulfide as a by-product of metabolism. Hydrogen sulfide results in a sulfur "rotten egg" odor at low tide. This sulfur odor is natural and does not signify pollution of tidal flats.

The hydrogen sulfide produced by anaerobic bacteria also accounts for the black color of tidal flat sediment. Iron in the mud reacts with hydrogen sulfide to form iron sulfides, which color the mud gray-black.

TIDES

In the Carolinas, ocean waters rise and fall twice in a 24-hour period — there are two high and two low tides daily.

Tides are mainly controlled by the moon, specifically the gravitational pull of the moon. Many other less important factors influence tides, and some factors remain yet unexplained.

Gravity is the mutual attraction of any two masses of matter. Gravitational pull is exerted on the earth's waters by the moon and the sun. Although the moon is much smaller than the sun, it is appreciably closer. As a result, the moon has a significantly larger effect on earth's tides.

The moon draws the closest ocean water toward itself. A high tide occurs at the earth's surface closest the moon and on the opposite side of the earth as well. Because the earth takes 24 hours to rotate on its axis, and the moon moves 1/29th of its orbit around the earth in 24 hours, high tide is 52 minutes later each day.

Other factors affecting tides include the sun's gravitational pull, onshore winds, atmospheric pressure, fresh water runoff, and water temperature (warm expands). Of these, the pull of the sun is reported to be the largest factor. In the Carolinas, at least, onshore winds have a very significant effect: Strong northeast winds result in higher tides.

When the moon, sun, and earth are in a straight line, the highest and lowest tides of the month occur (diagram 37). The moon is either new or full at this time. These wide-ranging (high-high and low-low) tides are called spring tides, not for the season, but for the tides "springing" forth. Similarly, low-ranging (low-high and high-low) tides occur when the moon and sun are at a right angle to the earth (diagram 38); then the pulls of the sun and moon work against each other. The moon is in mid-cycle at this time. These moderate tides are

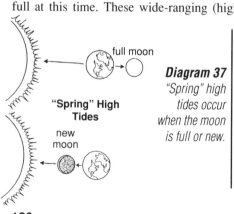

Diagram 37
"Spring" high tides occur when the moon is full or new.

"Spring" High Tides

full moon

new moon

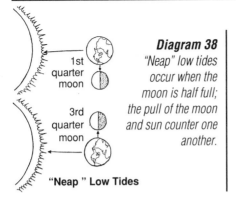

Diagram 38
*"Neap" low tides
occur when the
moon is half full;
the pull of the moon
and sun counter one
another.*

"Neap" Low Tides

called neap tides, meaning "hardly enough."

A wide range in heights of tides occurs over the surface of the earth. In some tropical areas, tides rise and fall less than a foot; at the Bay of Fundy in Canada, tides rise and fall 50 feet or more. In the Carolinas, tides range from 2 to 6 feet.

"Slack tide" or "slack water" is the interval at full high or low tide, when the direction of tidal flow is changing.

Low tide is the best time for beachcombers to explore the beach, or for clammers to rake clams: More area of the beach or mud flat is exposed.

WAVES

Almost everyone has seen waves on a lake or ocean. But what are waves? Aren't they just water crossing the surface of the ocean? What causes them? Why do waves "break" on the shore?

Waves are actually energy. Energy, not water, moves across the ocean's surface. Water particles only travel in a small circle as a wave passes.

The best way to understand waves as energy is to visualize a long rope laid on the ground. If a person picks up one end of the rope, and gives it a good snap, the rope behaves just like a wave on the ocean: The person applies energy at one end, and the energy moves down the rope. The rope itself does not move away from the person, but parts of the rope move up and down as the wave passes. The energy is released at the other end of the rope, just as the energy of waves is released on the shore.

In the case of oceanic waves, it is wind that provides energy. Wind causes a wave; the wave travels a distance in the ocean and then imparts its energy on a shoreline.

As waves travel, the distance between them increases, and they become more rounded. This explains why slow swells sometimes break on shore during a windless day: The swells were caused by winds up to thousands of miles away.

A wave breaks on the shore because the lower part of the wave hits the rising bottom of the shore first. The lower part is slowed, but the top keeps going; the top, or crest, "breaks" in front of the bottom of the wave. This wave-breaking process is similar to what happens when a beachcomber runs pell-mell into the ocean. The bottom half of the beachcomber is slowed by the water, but the top half of the beachcomber's body (in the air) keeps going and "breaks" headfirst into the water.

Wave terminology is simple. The distance between waves is the wave length. The distance from the crest (top) to the trough (lowest part between the waves) is the wave height.

Waves make beachcombing interesting. It is the energy of waves that washes shells, animals, and seaweed upon the shore.

SEAFOOD

NUTRITION

Benjamin Franklin was a man ahead of his time. The wise Franklin is known for many successful endeavors: discovering that lightning is electricity, co-authoring the Declaration of Independence, serving as ambassador to France and England, inventing the Franklin stove, and charting the Gulf Stream. A lesser-known accomplishment is Franklin's operation of several seafood markets in the Philadelphia area. Perhaps Franklin was ahead of his time promoting seafood, too!

Whether Ben Franklin knew it or not, one fact is clear: Seafood approaches being an ideal food. Seafood is high in protein, full of essential vitamins and minerals, yet low in calories and fat. Seafood is also low in cholesterol and higher in good-for-you polyunsaturated fats. Fresh seafood contains only small amounts of sodium chloride (salt). In addition, some fish oils may actually prevent heart disease.

Calories, in oversupply, cause obesity, one of the most serious health problems of Americans. Obesity may lead to heart disease, diabetes, and hypertension. Seafood provides tasty, yet low-calorie sustenance. An eight-ounce portion of Bluefish contains only 360 calories. Compare this with turkey at 590 calories and steak at 1,070 calories per eight ounces.

Protein, supplying the building blocks of life, is essential in humans' diet. Seafood is high in protein: An eight-ounce piece of flounder contains 45 grams of protein, about the same as eight ounces of steak.

Fat, the nutrient everyone tries to avoid, is present in low quantities in seafood. An eight-ounce serving of red snapper contains 7 grams of fat; eight ounces of shrimp contains 2 grams of fat. Quite a difference from an eight-ounce serving of "lean" ground beef, containing 23 grams of fat!

Cholesterol, the newest dietary "No-No," is present in seafood but in amounts less than in meat and poultry. Even shellfish have less cholesterol than previously believed. More accurate measurement techniques now available find 113 milligrams of cholesterol in eight ounces of oysters. Eight ounces of flounder has 157 milligrams of cholesterol, while an equal amount of lean ground beef has 197 milligrams.

Salt, or sodium chloride, is present in excessive amounts in most Americans' diets. Excessive salt is linked to hypertension (high blood pressure). One might think that seafood, fresh from the salty seas, is high in salt. Actually, the opposite is true: Fresh seafood contains relatively small amounts of sodium chloride.

These better-known, beneficial attributes provide only part of the healthful benefit of seafood consumption. Current research is investigating fish oils, the form of fat found in seafood. Fish oils contain omega-3 fatty acids, which may even protect high-risk persons from heart disease.

Speculation that fish omega-3 fatty acids exert a protective effect stems from observation of Greenland Eskimos. Despite a diet high in fat and cholesterol, the Eskimos have a low incidence of heart disease. In theory, fish the Eskimos consume provide omega-3 fatty acids, which protect them from heart disease.

While the healthful effects of fish oils are not proven, the evidence is suggestive. The possible protection from heart disease, along with proven nutritional qualities, make seafood an excellent food. The American Heart Association, in fact, recommends two to three meals of fish per week for prevention of heart disease.

WHICH SEAFOODS TASTE GOOD?

Seafood is a nearly ideal food. What kinds of seafood, then, are tasty enough to provide a healthy meal?

Everyone knows commonly eaten fish: grouper, snapper, flounder, seatrout, etc. Surprisingly, though, the species of fish and shellfish that can be enjoyed are almost limitless. Most any fish can be scrumptious, if properly prepared and cooked.

In order to enjoy various seafoods, one must first discard misconceptions, biases, and fishermens' tales about eating certain fish. Most fishermen and fish consumers forge opinions about the edibility of particular species from rumor or hearsay — rarely have they actually tried the fish themselves. Or, if they have eaten the fish, perhaps it was not fresh or not prepared properly after being caught.

As beauty is in the eye of the beholder, so is taste in the mouth of the eater. Many species considered to be "trash" fish in the U.S. are avidly sought by foreign seafood connoisseurs. Eel meat sells for $5 to $10 a pound in Europe. Shark meat is used in England's Fish and Chips. Lizard Fish are highly regarded in Southeast Asia. Squid and octopus are considered delicacies in parts of Europe and Asia. In Japan, mullet roe often sells for over $50 a pound!

Americans, in general, grossly underutilize seafood caught on our shores. This is not to say that Americans do not eat seafood — finicky Americans, partial to certain fish, overutilize imported fish. In 1987, the U.S. imported $8.7 billion in seafood products, while exports totaled only $1.6 billion. According to UNC Sea Grant, fishery products were second only to oil as a negative factor in the U.S. balance of trade! If Americans learned to better utilize their own species, the foreign trade imbalance might improve considerably.

The following fish are examples of perfectly edible species: pinfish, pigfish, eel, mullet, sea robin, amberjack, skates, rays, and sharks. Pinfish and pigfish fillets make great fish sandwiches. Eel is wonderful smoked. Skates, rays, and sharks, if handled properly, are excellent.

SEAFOOD BUYING/COOKING TIPS

Seafood is healthy for us, and there are numerous species from which to choose. What other factors are important in choosing and preparing seafood?

The three most important factors in choosing seafood are: fresh, fresh, and fresh. Fresh seafood simply cannot be surpassed. If someone says, "I don't like seafood," then that person has probably had a bad experience with non-fresh seafood.

How does one make sure seafood is fresh? First, shop where seafood can be seen, touched, and smelled. Don't shop where fish are hidden behind the counter. Next, learn how to spot fresh fish.

Probably the easiest way to tell if a fish is fresh is to look at its eyes: Are the eyes clear, bright, full, and lifelike (fresh)? Or are the eyes cloudy, dull, sunken, and lifeless (unfresh)? Gills also reveal whether a fish is fresh: Red gills without slime are fresh; brownish, slimy gills are not fresh. Finally, the nose knows: Smell a fish or container of scallops. Fresh seafood has a mild and pleasant odor, not an old and "fishy" one.

If you catch your own fish, be sure to ice the fish immediately after catching. Bluefish, amberjack, skates, rays, and sharks should all be bled (make a deep cut just above the tail), gutted and filleted, then iced as soon as possible.

When freezing fish, put the fish fillets in a container, and cover the fish with water. Freezing the fillets in a block of ice keeps them fresh-tasting.

Once you obtain fresh seafood, cook it properly. The biggest mistake in cooking seafood is overcooking. Overcooking causes seafood to lose its melt-in-your-mouth, delicious taste, turning it dry, rubbery, and tasteless.

Follow cooking times in recipes closely. As a rough estimate, allow ten minutes of cooking per inch thickness of fish. Test the fish frequently to see if it's done; when fish flakes easily, it's ready to eat.

Shrimp, too, tastes best if cooked briefly — about three minutes or less if boiled.

Cook seafood by broiling, baking, boiling, steaming, or grilling; these cooking methods retain the nutritional qualities of seafood. Frying seafood, on the other hand, often adds calories and fat that offset the nutritional benefits of seafood. For instance, McDonald's Filet-O-Fish sandwich has a bit more fat and calories than McDonald's Quarter Pounder Hamburger!

So, be wise like Ben Franklin: Eat seafood. Any seafood will do, as long as it's fresh. Enjoy the great taste, and, at the same time, do your health a favor.

AUTHOR'S COMMENTS

THE ENVIRONMENT

Man has been here almost no time at all. Yet he is rapidly making the world less fit for life — including his own. Will the human story amount to even a page of time in the history book of the earth?

The above quote is inscribed on a roadside marker in Dinosaur National Monument, Utah. In this fascinating park, the fossilized bones of dinosaurs bring the Age of Dinosaurs to life. One realizes that dinosaurs were real — not just pictures in books or toys our children collect. Dinosaurs dominated the earth for 140 million years!

Why did these behemoths perish? And, as the sign asks, will humans go the way of dinosaurs, only much more quickly? Are we not smart enough to anticipate and plan our future? Are we not caring and clever enough to control our destiny?

It is agonizingly clear that we have yet to grasp the potential impact of our power. The capability of drastically altering earth's environment is a relatively recent development, appearing with modern technology. The technology explosion is far outstripping our ability to comprehend the effects of such advances.

Modern man must change his basic attitudes if the human race is to survive: Like the American Indians, today's people must adopt the concept that humans are a part of nature, not its subduer or conqueror. We must understand that any action of ours that has a significant effect upon the environment will eventually affect us in some way as well.

If we fail to change, we should place ourselves on the Endangered Species List. For surely, humans will extinguish themselves if they cannot adapt.

IT'S TIME TO:

- Recycle in earnest.
- Drive fuel-efficient cars; own and operate fewer vehicles.
- Build bikeways, ride bikes.
- Preserve more natural areas.
- Build and buy small, well-insulated homes.
- Reduce meat consumption, especially beef.
- Conserve electricity instead of drilling oil in fragile environments.
- Intensify research on clean energy sources.
- Practice and promote birth control (stop overpopulating).
- Store trash and toxic wastes safely.
- Plan for the long-term instead of the short-term.
- Take care of our planet earth!

• • •

OLD:

Be faithful, and multiply, and replenish the earth, and subdue it. And have dominion over the fish of the sea, and over the fowl of the air, and over every living thing that moveth upon the face of the earth.

We've done this, so let's get on with the

NEW:

Be responsible, and control human population; revere the earth, and live in harmony with it. Respect the fish of the oceans, the birds of the air, and every other living thing on earth.

CONSERVATION NOTES

Dredge-spoil islands are under-appreciated areas of crucial importance to many coastal bird species. These man-made islands are created when river channels (to ports), the intracoastal waterway, or inlets are dredged. Sand is pumped out of the channels and piled onto mounds adjacent to the channels.

The islands provide ideal nesting habitats for egrets, gulls, terns, skimmers, herons, and ibises. A 1979 North Carolina study (Parnell and Soots) found almost 80 percent of these colonial-nesting waterbirds nesting on man-made or man-modified sites! Formerly, the birds nested on natural estuarine or barrier islands, many of which have been lost to development.

The birds' "last stand" nesting areas must be respected. The dredge-spoil nesting sites should be left alone. If a colony of birds is encroached upon by mistake, the cries and feigned attacks of the disturbed birds should be heeded: Leave as quickly as possible.

● ● ●

Fishing line left in the environment can be devastating to birds. Birds can become entangled in the strand; a broken leg, crippled wing, or strangulation may result. An entangled bird may even fly back to its nesting site and entangle other birds in the same line.

Used fishing line should be cut up and placed in the garbage, not left carelessly in the environment.

● ● ●

The practice of throwing unwanted fish on the beach or pier to die is an outdated practice, a needless waste. All creatures, be they sharks, stingrays, toadfish, puffers, eels, or others, have a place and purpose in the world (many of these fish are actually edible, too).

Responsible fishermen release unwanted fish back into the water. All fishermen should adopt this practice. Pier operators can help by posting signs requesting that all unwanted fish be released.

● ● ●

ATV/four-wheel drive vehicles should be used with care at the beach. Vehicles must stay off the dunes: Dune plants, which stabilize the dunes, and nesting birds are disturbed and killed by vehicular traffic.

Conscientious ATV users must help keep irresponsible ATV users off the dunes. If "bad apple" ATVers abuse the dunes, all vehicle traffic on the beach will be prohibited.

ANOTHER COMMON SPECIES: TOUROID

Touroids, also known as "Spuds" or "Gringos," are people who visit the beach on vacation. Touroids are seasonally abundant on the Carolina coast; they gather in greatest numbers between Memorial Day and Labor Day. No single characteristic absolutely identifies a Touroid, but one or more of the following signs suggests a positive Touroid sighting:

- Walking to the beach overburdened with towels, blankets, beach umbrellas, coolers, rafts, chairs, beachballs, radios, shovels, buckets, etc.

- Beach towels soaked by waves (from placing them too close to the surf during an incoming tide)

- Spending endless hours walking up and down the beach, collecting worthless shells

- Wearing loud Hawaiian print shirts, funky shorts, weird hats

- Wearing socks with sandals, or socks with any type of shoes during the summer

- Talking with a foreign-sounding accent; inability to understand local beach dialect

- Buying or sending multiple sets of postcards

- Asking directions for the fourth time to the same destination

- Driving down one-way streets the wrong way

- Driving 10 mph (the speed of a turtle) in a 35 mph zone, gawking at the sights

- Buying shells, trinkets, and souvenirs in tourist-trap shops

- Invariably ordering seafood platters in restaurants

- Appearance in the evening with a lobster-red sunburn (after roasting on the beach all day long)

Note: The author freely admits to being a Touroid on many occasions.

FACTS FOR THOUGHT

- Dragonflies are helpful to man — they eat mosquitoes.
- Oysters change sex repeatedly during their lives. Groupers start life as females and later become males.
- Clams, oysters, Menhaden, the largest fish on earth (Whale Shark), the largest animal <u>ever</u> on earth (Blue Whale), and other baleen whales — what do all these animals have in common?
  Answer: They are filter feeders. They strain sea water to feed on tiny plant and animal life.
- Sea stars use a hydraulic (water pipe/pump) system for movement instead of muscles.
- Find a shell riddled with hundreds of tiny holes? It was likely the victim of a boring sponge or marine worms. Orange-colored sponges attach to a shell and secrete an acid substance that eats through the shell. Marine worms bore tunnels through the shell.
- What has five eyes and hundreds of feet? Answer: a sea star (starfish). Sea stars have an eye at the end of each of their five arms and move on hundreds of tube feet on their underside.
- The organism that causes the Red Tide, *Ptychodiscus brevis*, is sometimes called an alga, sometimes a protozoa. An alga is a plant, a protozoa an animal. Why the confusion? *Ptychodiscus brevis* is a dinoflagellate: Dinoflagellates possess the capacity to photosynthesize — a decidedly plant-like behavior. Dinoflagellates also possess flagella, enabling them to move about on their own — definitely an animal (protozoan) characteristic.
- North Carolina's state seashell is the Scotch Bonnet. The state fish is the Red Drum.
- South Carolina's state seashell is the Lettered Olive and the state fish is the Striped Bass.
- The shrimp we eat have something in common with people. They come in three different colors: pink, brown, and white!
- Sharks, rays, and skates have copulatory organs, and copulate.
- A female Blue Crab mates only one time in her life; this single mating lasts six to twelve hours.
- Living coral resembles a plant. The structure is actually a colony of tiny animals. Ironically, the coral polyps are dependent on plants (single-celled algae) living within their bodies.
- Horseshoe Crabs have been swimming in the oceans since <u>before</u> dinosaurs ever roamed the earth.

QUOTES OF NOTE

"Study nature, not books."
  —*Louis Agassiz, 19th century naturalist*

"He was a very valiant man who first adventured in eating of oysters."
  —*Thomas Fuller, 1608-1661*

"He was a bold man that first eat an oyster."
  —*Jonathan Swift, author*

"If you are not an environmentalist, you are either selfish or ignorant."
  —*Andwar Bundini, M.D., physician and philosopher*

"A man may fish with the worm that hath eat of a king, and eat of the fish that hath fed of that worm."
  —*William Shakespeare, Hamlet*

"Old proverb says,
That bird is not honest
That filleth his own nest."
  —*John Shelton c. 1460-1529*

"New proverb says,
That man is not wise
That fouleth his own earth."
  —*Andwar Bundini, contemporary metaphysician*

"Third Fisherman: Master, I marvel how the fishes live in the sea.
First Fisherman: Why, as men do a-land: the great ones eat up the little ones."
  —*William Shakespeare, Pericles, Prince of Tyre*

SCIENTIFIC NAMES

BIRDS:
Black Skimmer
Rynchops niger
Brown Pelican
Pelecanus occidentalis
Cormorant
Phalacrocorax auritus
Great Egret
Casmerodius albus
Snowy Egret
Egretta thula
Laughing Gull
Larus atricilla
Herring Gull
Larus argentatus
Ring-billed Gull
Larus delawarensis
Great Blue Heron
Ardea herodias
Tricolored Heron
Hydranassa tricolor
Green-backed Heron
Butorides striatus
Mallard Duck
Anas platyrhynchos
Osprey
Pandion haliaetus
Oystercatcher
Haematopus palliatus
Ruddy Turnstone
Arenaria interpres
Sanderling
Calidris alba
Least Tern
Sterna albifrons.
Common Tern
Sterna hirundo
Royal Tern
Sterna maxima
Caspian Tern
Sterna caspia
White Ibis
Eudocimus albus
Willet
*Catoptrophorus
semipalmatus*

CRABS AND CRUSTACEANS:
Blue Crab
Callinectes sapidus
Fiddler Crab
Uca species
Ghost Crab
Ocypode quadrata
Hermit Crab
Clibanarius species
Pagurus species
Horseshoe Crab
Limulus polyphemus
Marsh Crab
Sesarma species
Oyster Crab
Pinnotheres ostreum
Stone Crab
Menippe mercenaria
Acorn Barnacle
Balanus species
Goose Barnacle
Lepas species
Mole Crab
Emerita talpoida
Shrimp
Penaeus species
Spiny Lobster
Panulirus argus

SHELLS (MOLLUSKS):
Angel Wing
Cyrtopleura costata
Ark Shell
Anadara species
Auger Shell
Terebra species
Clam (Quahog)
Mercenaria mercenaria
Cockle, Giant Atlantic
Dinocardium robustum
Coquina Clam
Donax variabilis
Cross-barred Venus Clam
Chione cancellata

Disk Shell
Dosinia species
Jingle Shell
Anomia simplex
Keyhole Limpet
Diodora cayenensis
Kitten's Paw
Plicatula gibbosa
Marsh Periwinkle
Littorina irrorata
Moon Shell (Shark Eye)
Polinices duplicatus
Mud Snail
Ilyanassa obsoleta
Ribbed Mussel
Geukensia demissa
Blue Mussel
Mytilus edulis
Olive Shell
Oliva sayana
Oyster, Eastern
Crassostrea virginica
Oyster Drill
Urosalpinx cinerea
Pen Shell
Atrina species
Atlantic Jackknife Clam
Ensis directus
Razor Clams, Tagelus
Tagelus species
Scallop
Argopecten species
Scotch Bonnet
Phalium granulatum
Slipper Shell
Crepidula species
Sundial
Architectonica nobilis
Surf Clam
Spisula solidissima
Banded Tulip
Fasciolaria hunteria
Fasciolaria lilium
True Tulip
Fasciolaria tulipa

SCIENTIFIC NAMES

Turkey Wing
Arca zebra
Lightning Whelk
Busycon contrarium
Channeled Whelk
Busycon canaliculatum
Knobbed Whelk
Busycon carica
Worm Shell
Vermicularia knorri

FISH:
Bluefish
Pomatomus saltatrix
Burrfish
Chilomycterus species
Puffer
Sphoeroides species
Croaker
*Micropogonias
undulatus*
Eel
Anguilla rostrata
Flounder
Paralichthys species
Kingfish (Whiting)
Menticirrhus species
Lizard Fish
Synodus species
King Mackerel
Scomberomorus cavalla
Spanish Mackerel
*Scomberomorus
maculatus*
Menhaden
Brevoortia tyrannus
Mullet
Mugil species
Oyster Toadfish
Opsanus tau
Pigfish
Orthopristis chrysoptera
Pinfish
Lagodon rhomboides
Pompano
Trachinotus carolinus

Red Drum
Sciaenops ocellatus
Seatrout
Cynoscion nebulosus
Atlantic Sharpnose Shark
*Rhizoprionodon
terraenovae*
Smooth Dogfish Shark
Mustelus canis
Spiny Dogfish Shark
Squalus acanthias
Sheepshead
*Archosargus
probatocephalus*
Skate
Raja species
Stingray
Dasyatis species
Spot
Leiostomus xanthurus

OTHERS:
Anole
Anolis carolinensis
Argiope spider
Argiope species
Coral, Ivory Bush
Oculina species
Coral, Star
Astrangia species
Cannonball Jellyfish
Stomolophus meleagris
Portuguese Man-of-War
Physalia physalis
Sand Dollar, Keyhole
*Mellita
quinquiesperforata*
Sea Lettuce
Ulva lactuca
Sea Star (Starfish)
Asterias forbesi
Loggerhead Turtle
Caretta caretta
Purple Sea Urchin
Arbacia punctulata

White Sea Urchin
Lytechinus variegatus
Shipworm
*Teredo or Bankia
species*
Touroid
Homo sapiens weirdus

COASTAL ENVIRONMENT:
Beach Grass
Ammophila breviligulata
Eel Grass
Zostera marina
Marsh Grass
Spartina species
Sea Oats
Uniola paniculata

140

RECOMMENDED READING

Amos, William H., and Stephen H. Amos. *The Audubon Society Nature Guides, Atlantic and Gulf Coasts*. New York: Alfred A. Knopf, Inc., 1987.

Audubon Society Field Guide to North American Fishes, Whales, and Dolphins. New York: Alfred A. Knopf, Inc., 1983.

Ballantine, Todd. *Tideland Treasure*. Hilton Head Island, South Carolina: Deerfield Publishing, 1983.

Cartmell, B. Clay. *Let's Go Fossil Shark Tooth Hunting*. Ann Arbor, Michigan: Natural Science Research, 1978.

Coulombe, Deborah A. *The Seaside Naturalist*. New York: Prentice Hall Press, 1987.

Ehrlich, Anne H., and Paul R. Ehrlich. *Earth*. New York: Franklin Watts, Inc., 1987.

Farrard, John, Jr. *The Audubon Society Master Guide to Birding*. New York: Alfred A. Knopf, Inc., 1983.

Gosner, Kenneth L. *A Field Guide to the Atlantic Seashore, The Peterson Field Guide Series*. Boston: Houghton Mifflin Co., 1986.

Groves, Don. *The Oceans: A Book of Questions and Answers*. New York: John Wiley and Sons, Inc., 1989.

Hersey, John. *Blues*. New York: Random House, Inc., 1987.

Kaplan, Eugene H. *Peterson Field Guides, Southeastern and Caribbean Seashores*. Boston: Houghton Mifflin Co., 1988.

Kopper, Philip. *The Wild Edge, Life and Lore of the Great Atlantic Beaches*. New York: Penguin Books, 1981.

Manooch, Charles S., III. *Fisherman's Guide, Fishes of the Southeastern United States*. Raleigh, NC: NC State Museum of Natural History, 1988.

Mason, Phillip. *Shellfish Cookbook*. New York: Drake Publishers, Inc., 1974.

Meinkoth, Norman A. *The Audubon Society Field Guide to North American Seashore Creatures*. New York: Alfred A Knopf, Inc., 1981.

Parnell, James F., and Robert F. Soots, Jr. *Atlas of Colonial Waterbirds of North Carolina Estuaries*. Raleigh, North Carolina: UNC Sea Grant Publication, 1979.

Pearson, Thomas Gilbert, and Clement Samuel Brimley and Herbert Hutchison Brimley. *Birds of North Carolina*. Raleigh, NC: Bynum Printing Co., 1942.

RECOMMENDED READING

Perry, Bill. *A Sierra Club Naturalist's Guide to The Middle Atlantic Coast, Cape Hatteras to Cape Cod*. San Francisco: Sierra Club Books, 1985.

Pilkey, Orrin H. Jr. *From Currituck to Calabash, Living With North Carolina's Barrier Islands*. Durham, North Carolina: Duke University Press, 1980.

Porter, Hugh J., and Jim Tyler. *Seashells Common to North Carolina*. North Carolina: UNC-Sea Grant, 1981.

Potter, Eloise F., and James F. Parnell, and Robert P. Teulings. *Birds of the Carolinas*. Chapel Hill, North Carolina: The University of North Carolina Press, 1980.

Rehder, Harald A. *The Audubon Society Field Guide to North American Seashells*. New York: Alfred A Knopf, Inc., 1981.

Rhyne, Nancy. *Carolina Seashells*. Charlotte, North Carolina: Fast and McMillan Publishers, Inc., 1982.

Robins, C. Richard, and G. Carleton Ray. *The Peterson Field Guide Series, A Field Guide to Atlantic Coast Fishes of North America*. Boston: Houghton Mifflin Co., 1986.

Ruppert, Edward E., and Richard S. Fox. *Seashore Animals of the Southeast*. Columbia, South Carolina: University of South Carolina Press, 1988.

Schwartz, Frank J., and Jim Tyler. *Marine Fishes Common to North Carolina*. North Carolina: Department of Natural Resources, 1970.

Schwartz, Frank J. *Sharks of North Carolina and Adjacent Waters*. private printing. 1979.

Schwartz, Frank J. *Sharks, Sawfish, Skates, and Rays of the Carolinas*. Morehead City, N.C: Institute of Marine Sciences, 1984.

Southern Seafood Classics. Atlanta, Georgia: Peachtree Publishers, Ltd., 1988.

Spitsbergen, Judith M. *Seacoast Life, An Ecological Guide to Natural Seashore Communities in North Carolina*. Chapel Hill, North Carolina: The University of North Carolina Press, 1983.

Spitsbergen, Judith M. *Strange Seafood Recipes*. North Carolina: Herald Printing Company, 1982.

Weiner, Jonathan. *Planet Earth*. New York: Bantam Books, 1986.

Zinn, Donald J. *The Handbook for Beach Strollers from Maine to Cape Hatteras*. Chester, Connecticut: The Globe Pequot Press, 1975.

DEFINITIONS

adductor muscle: muscle pulling the two parts of a clam-like bivalve closed

aerobic: with oxygen

algae: simple plants without roots, stems, leaves, or flowers; microscopic to large in size

anaerobic: without oxygen

barrier island: a long, usually narrow island that parallels the coastal mainland

bilateral symmetry: animal with two equal body halves on either side of a line dividing its body; humans exhibit bilateral symmetry

bivalve: clam-like mollusk with a two-part shell

brackish: water of intermediate salt content, between fresh and sea water; sea water that has been diluted with fresh water

byssal threads: thin fibers secreted by some bivalves; the threads attach the bivalves to the bottom

carapace: in crustaceans, the part of the outer shell (exoskeleton) covering the thorax

carnivore: an animal that feeds on other animals (flesheater)

carrion: decaying flesh of a dead animal

crustacean: invertebrate (no backbone) animal with segmented body, jointed legs, stalked eyes, and a hard external shell

detritus: small pieces of decaying plant and animal matter

dredge-spoil island: man-made island created when sand is dredged out of the intracoastal waterway, inlet, or river channel; crucial nesting habitat for many coastal bird species

estuary: area where a freshwater river meets the saltwater ocean, forming brackish water of intermediate salinity; loosely used to mean any coastal water of salinity between ocean and fresh water

exoskeleton: external shell used by an animal for protection, support, and muscle attachment

gastropod: snail-like mollusk with one-part shell

gill: breathing organ of fish; extracts oxygen from the water

gill rakers: finger-like projections off gills; in most species rakers clean the surfaces of the gill filaments; in some species, adapted to filter water passing over the gills, collecting food

habitat: the area in which an animal lives

herbivore: an animal that feeds on plants

holdfast: a structure used to hold an animal or plant to the bottom, hard substrate, or plant leaves

DEFINITIONS

hydroid: small animals with tubular bodies, attached on one end, fuzzy tentacles on the other end; hydroids grow in dense, flower-like colonies on rock or wood surfaces

invertebrate: animal without a backbone or spinal cord; all animals except fish, amphibians, reptiles, birds, and mammals

larva: immature form of an animal which changes shape before becoming an adult

mammal: vertebrate animal with mammary (milk) glands and hair at some time in its life

mantle: in mollusks, the tissue sac that surrounds the internal organs and secretes the shell

marine: pertaining to the ocean

marsh: grassy area periodically flooded by water

metamorphosis: change in body form during development of an animal

mollusk: invertebrate animals with soft bodies surrounded by shells; includes clam-like bivalves and snail-like gastropods

molt: process by which an animal sheds and regrows its external skeleton

nematocyst: stinging cell of jellyfish and similar animals

neap tide: low-ranging tides

nocturnal: active at night

omnivore: an animal that feeds on both plants and animals

OSEND: Ocean-Spawned, Estuarine-Nursery Dependent; fish or other animal species with eggs laid in the ocean and larvae that migrate to the estuarine marsh system for their initial growth

operculum: lid-like covering; in snails, round horny plate that closes the opening to the shell; in fish, bony plate that covers the gills

pectoral fins: paired fins near the gill covers of a fish

pelvic fins: paired fins on the underside of a fish

periostracum: a thin outer layer covering some shells; can be smooth or hairy

phylum: a large, basic division of the plant or animal kingdoms

phytoplankton: plant plankton

plankton: aquatic plants and animals that float at the mercy of tides and currents; most are microscopic; includes phytoplankton (plants) and zooplankton (animals)

proboscis: in snail-like gastropods, a tube-like extension of the head, used in feeding

radial symmetry: animal with equal body parts radiating from a central point, like a pie cut into equal pieces; sea stars, sand dollars, and sea urchins exhibit five-part radial symmetry

DEFINITIONS

radula: in snail-like gastropods, a toothed, tongue-like structure used for tearing, rasping, boring, or chewing

salinity: the saltiness of water, measured in parts per thousand

scavenger: an animal that feeds on dead plants and animals

school: large group of similar aquatic animals swimming together

seaweed: marine plants; most are algae

sessile: permanently attached, immobile; a sessile animal does not move about in its environment

shellfish: strictly speaking, any aquatic invertebrate animal with a shell, especially the edible species such as lobster, crabs, clams, and oysters; newer usage refers only to bivavle mollusks such as clams and oysters, as when an area is closed to taking shellfish (refers to clams and oysters, not crabs)

species: a basic, distinct category of plants or animals; the members of a species are able to interbreed

spring tide: high-ranging tides; occur in association with new and full moons

substrate: solid surface upon which an animal attaches or lives; typically rocks, wood, man-made structures, shells, etc.

surf zone: area where waves break on ocean beaches; moves up and down the beach with rising and falling tides

tide: bi-daily rise and fall in ocean level along coasts

toxin: poisonous substance

vertebrate: animal with a backbone and spinal cord; includes fish, amphibians, reptiles, birds, and mammals

warm-blooded: homeothermic, or having a relatively constant, controlled, warm internal body temperature; birds and mammals are warm-blooded

zooplankton: animal plankton

INDEX

Bold numbers indicate corresponding pictures.

146

ABOUT THE AUTHOR

Peter Meyer is a naturalist with an insatiable curiosity about the environment. Meyer's keen interest in his surroundings motivates him to explore, investigate, and learn everything he can about the plants, animals and ecosystems of the coast.

While searching for books about the coast, the author was unable to find a practical, all-encompassing guide to the Carolina coastal environment. Meyer decided to undertake the task of filling this literary void. *Nature Guide to the Carolina Coast* is the culmination of more than five years of efforts — accumulating information, gathering and photographing specimens, writing, rewriting, and writing again.

Meyer has a strong academic background. He received a Bachelor of Arts degree in zoology from Miami (Ohio) University, where he was elected to Phi Beta Kappa. Meyer subsequently received a Doctor of Medicine degree from Ohio State University, where he was elected to Alpha Omega Alpha (another academic honorary).

For the past ten years, Dr. Meyer has practiced medicine in Wilmington, North Carolina. He is a board-certified emergency physician. Meyer resides in Wilmington with his wife, Cathy, and sons, Benjamin Cetacean and Jason Avian.

Aside from medicine, Meyer enjoys running, reading, fishing, photography, scuba diving, preparing seafood, and, last but not least, writing. Through writing, the author hopes to foster respect and concern for the environment, especially among younger readers.

NATURE GUIDE TO THE
CAROLINA COAST

can be ordered by mail.

Books ordered by mail are shipped promptly.

Every book ordered by mail is
signed by the author.

Books can be personalized, too.
Print legibly the name of the person(s) to whom
the book is to be signed
(for example, "to Bob and Sally").

Personalize to:

Order form

Send a check or money order only.

Name _____

Address_____

City_____State_____Zip_____

Send _____ copies of *Nature Guide* at $13.95 _____

Shipping for the first book $2.00 _____

Shipping for each additional book $ .50 _____

NC residents add tax per copy of $ .84 _____

Total _____

Make checks payable to **Avian-Cetacean Press**

Mail to: **Avian-Cetacean Press**
PO Box 15643, Wilmington, NC 28408

FIELD NOTES